C000171390

ROUGH MAGIC PRESENTS THE WORLD PREMIÈRE OF

TAKE ME AWAY

BY GERALD MURPHY

TAKE ME AWAY RECEIVED ITS WORLD PREMIÈRE
AT PROJECT ARTS CENTRE, DUBLIN, ON 13TH FEBRUARY 2004

THE PLAY WAS STAGED AS PART OF **ROUGH MAGIC IN REP,** RUNNING IN REPERTORY
WITH **WORDS OF ADVICE FOR YOUNG PEOPLE** BY IOANNA ANDERSON

ROUGH MAGIC PRESENTS THE WORLD PREMIÈRE OF

TAKE ME AWAY
BY GERALD MURPHY

CAST [IN ORDER OF APPEARANCE]

BREN	**JOE HANLEY**	DIRECTOR	**LYNNE PARKER**
ANDY	**AIDAN KELLY**	SET DESIGNER	**ALAN FARQUHARSON**
KEV	**BARRY WARD**	COSTUME DESIGNER	**EIMER NÍ MHAOLDOMHNAIGH**
EDDIE	**VINCENT McCABE**	LIGHTING DESIGNER	**JOHN COMISKEY**
		PRODUCTION MANAGER	**MARIE BREEN**
		STAGE DIRECTOR	**AISLING MOONEY**
		STAGE DIRECTOR	**PAULA TIERNEY**
		STAGE MANAGER	**JUSTIN MURPHY**
		PROPS BUYER	**BREEGE BRENNAN**
		PRODUCTION ELECTRICIAN	**JOE GLASGOW**
		SOUND	**CORMAC CARROLL**
		SET CONSTRUCTION	**THEATRE PRODUCTION SERVICES**
		SCENIC ARTIST	**LIZ BARKER**
		GRAPHIC DESIGN	**ALPHABET SOUP**
		PUBLICIST	**PAUL FAHY**
		MARKETING ASSISTANT	**NICOLE BRENNAN-O'DWYER**
		ADMINISTRATOR	**ELIZABETH WHYTE**
		PRODUCER	**LOUGHLIN DEEGAN**

The performance runs for approximately 90 minutes without an interval.

TAKE ME AWAY was commissioned and developed during the **SEEDS** new writing project, a joint initiative between Rough Magic Theatre Company and the Dublin Fringe Festival.

ROUGH MAGIC WOULD LIKE TO THANK THE FOLLOWING FOR THEIR KIND ASSISTANCE:
The Arts Council of Ireland, Mike Bradwell, Des Cave, Phelim Drew, David Herlihy, Darragh Kelly, Deirdre Molloy, Tomás Ó Suilleabhain, Ali Curran, Kerry West, Vallejo Gantner, Scott Watson, Dublin City Council, and all the staff of Project Arts Centre.

Please note that the text of the play which appears in this volume may be changed during the rehearsal process and appear in slightly altered form in performance.

ROUGH MAGIC AND NEW WRITING

The core of Rough Magic's work is the development and production of new work for the stage. Founded in 1984, the company began by presenting Irish premières of major plays from the contemporary international scene, before beginning to commission and develop new plays from Irish writers. Throughout the nineties, the company presented plays by a number of significant writers including Declan Hughes, Gina Moxley, Donal O'Kelly and Arthur Riordan. In the early nineties the company initiated a timely women's writing project which led to the production of plays by Pom Boyd and Paula Meehan. Six of these writers' debut plays were collected in Rough Magic: First Plays (New Island Books, 1999).

"Few companies set the stage ablaze quite like Rough Magic" Time Out

Following the establishment of a dedicated Literary Department in 2001, the company initiated the highly successful **SEEDS** project, in association with the Dublin Fringe Festival. **SEEDS** was established to seek out, encourage, enable, develop and stage new Irish writing. After a rigorous selection process, six emerging writers were chosen for commission. The six writers were Ioanna Anderson, Mark Doherty, Aidan Harney, Oonagh Kearney, Gerald Murphy and Raymond Scannell. Each writer was assigned a mentor from a group of highly experienced international directors – Mike Bradwell, Philip Howard, Wilson Milam, Conall Morrison, Jim Nolan and Max Stafford-Clark. Each play was developed over a twelve-month period, supported by workshops and private readings, and all six were presented as a series of public readings in 2002, followed by a seminar on new writing initiatives in Ireland. The **ROUGH MAGIC in REP** presentation of **Words of Advice for Young People** by Ioanna Anderson and **Take Me Away** by Gerald Murphy, brings to four the number of **SEEDS** plays that have subsequently received full productions. A fifth is being considered for a possible production in 2004/2005.

Rough Magic will be initiating a new phase of the project, **SEEDS 2**, in 2004. Alongside support for emerging Irish writers, the new programme will also provide a development programme for emerging Irish directors.

"It is a measure of Rough Magic's success over the years that when it launches a new production, one automatically sits up and takes notice" Irish Times

In addition to the **SEEDS** project, Rough Magic continues to commission, develop and present new plays by leading Irish playwrights. Recent productions include **Shiver** by Declan Hughes (2003) and **Midden** by Morna Regan (Fringe First Award, Edinburgh Fringe Festival, 2001). At any one time, the company's rolling programme of new play commissions includes a diverse range of work at various stages of development, and we currently have six new pieces in progress for future production. The Literary Department also reads, discusses and responds to the many unsolicited scripts submitted for consideration, and provides feedback and encouragement to promising playwrights on an ongoing basis.

Further information on Rough Magic is available at **www.rough-magic.com**

GERALD MURPHY WRITER

Gerald Murphy's first full-length play, **The Welcome**, was presented by Druid Theatre Company in 2001 as part of their Druid Debuts series. **Take Me Away** was developed during the **SEEDS** project, produced by Rough Magic in association with the Dublin Fringe Festival, and was given a staged reading in 2002. His first radio play, **Stranger in the Night**, was broadcast by RTÉ in 2001 and won an RTÉ PJ O'Connor award. **Take Me Away** was also adapted for radio and broadcast by RTÉ in 2002 and a further radio play, **Seer Point**, was commissioned and broadcast by RTÉ in November 2003. In addition to his theatre work, Gerald has written episodes for RTÉ's long-running drama series, **Fair City**. Gerald also works as a script development consultant for film and animation.

LYNNE PARKER DIRECTOR

Lynne is co-founder and Artistic Director of Rough Magic Theatre Company and an Associate Director of the Abbey Theatre.

Productions for Rough Magic include **Top Girls, Decadence, The Country Wife, Nightshade, Spokesong, Serious Money, Aunt Dan and Lemon, The Tempest, Tom and Viv, Lady Windermere's Fan, Digging For Fire, Love And A Bottle, I Can't Get Started, New Morning, Danti Dan, Down Onto Blue, The Dogs, Hidden Charges, Halloween Night, The Way Of The World, Pentecost, Northern Star, The School for Scandal, The Whisperers, Boomtown, Three Days Of Rain, Dead Funny, Midden, Copenhagen** (Best Production, 2002 Irish Times/ESB Irish Theatre Awards), **Shiver** and **Olga**.

Productions at the Abbey and Peacock Theatres include **The Trojan Women, The Doctor's Dilemma, Tartuffe, Down the Line, The Sanctuary Lamp, The Drawer Boy** (Galway Arts Festival co-production) and **The Shape of Metal**.

Other work outside the company includes productions for Druid, Tinderbox, Opera Theatre Company and 7:84 Scotland, and Lynne was an associate artist of Charabanc for whom she adapted and directed **The House of Bernarda Alba**. Lynne has also directed **The Clearing** (Bush Theatre); **The Playboy of the Western World, The Silver Tassie** and **Our Father** (Almeida Theatre); **Brothers of the Brush** (Arts Theatre); **The Shadow of a Gunman** (Gate, Dublin); **Playhouse Creatures** (The Peter Hall Company at the Old Vic); **The Importance of Being Earnest** (West Yorkshire Playhouse); **Love Me?!** (Corn Exchange's Car Show); **The Comedy of Errors** (RSC); **Olga** (Traverse Theatre, Edinburgh) and **The Drunkard** (B*spoke Theatre Company).

JOE HANLEY BREN

Formerly a member of Dublin Youth Theatre, Joe made his professional acting debut with Rough Magic in Caryl Churchill's **Serious Money** in 1988. Other theatre credits include: **Twelve Angry Men** and **One Flew Over The Cuckoo's Nest** (Lane Productions); **Rap Éire** and **Much Ado About Nothing** (Bickerstaffe); **The Plough and the Stars** (Gaiety); **The Importance of Being Earnest** (Town Hall Theatre); **As You Like It** (Druid); **Massive Damages** (Passion Machine); **The Playboy of the Western World, As You Like It** and **Macbeth** (Second Age) and **Romeo and Juliet** (Gate). Television and film credits include: **Fair City** (RTÉ); **Michael Collins; Run of the Country; Agnes Brown; Flick; The Count of Monto Cristo; How Harry Became a Tree; Veronica Guerin** and **Adam and Paul.**

AIDAN KELLY ANDY

This is Aidan's first appearance with Rough Magic. Other theatre credits include: **The Good Father** and **Philadelphia, Here I Come!** (Druid); **The Plough and The Stars, The Barbaric Comedies** and **Juno and the Paycock** (Abbey); **Women In Arms** (Storytellers); **Diarmuid and Gráinne** and **The Dublin Trilogy** (Passion Machine); **Howie the Rookie** (The Bush Theatre/Assembly Rooms, Edinburgh/PS 122, New York); **Comedians** (Andrews Lane); **Zoe's Play** (The Ark); **The Shaughran** (Edinburgh Lyceum); **Much Ado About Nothing** (Bickerstaffe); **The Dead School** (Macnas) and **Sucking Dublin** (Peacock). Radio credits include: **O'Flatherty's Window** and **Stopping the Rising** (BBC Radio 4). Television and film credits include: **Bachelor's Walk, The Cassidys, Making the Cut** and **Fair City** (RTÉ); **The Birthday; On The Edge; Dullisc; Majella McGinty; Durangoa** and **Michael Collins.**

VINCENT McCABE EDDIE

This is Vincent's first appearance with Rough Magic. Previous theatre credits include: **Juno and the Paycock** and **Tarry Flynn** (Abbey); **Asylum, Asylum, Buried Child,** and **The Wild Duck** (Peacock); **Famine** (Druid); **Unless it goes on beyond the Grave, The Liberty Suit, The Risen People** and **Bent** (Project); **Buddleia** (Passion Machine/Olympia); **Brothers of the Brush** (Arts Theatre London); **Burke and Blake** (Focus); **Rosie and Starwars** (Calypso) and **Sixteen Words for Water** (Crypt). Film and television credits include: **Bad Karma; Alice in Chains; Ballykissangel; Bachelor's Walk; The Butcher Boy; Durango; Flick; Fair City; Family; Glenroe; Into the West; Lapsed Catholics; Michael Collins; Nora; Not Afraid, Not Afraid** and **Pigs.**

BARRY WARD KEV

Barry first appeared with Rough Magic in the **SEEDS** reading of **Take Me Away.** Other theatre credits include: **The Lieutenant of Inishmore** (Royal Shakespeare Company UK tour/Dublin Theatre Festival); **Sive** (Druid/Gaiety); **A Whistle in the Dark** (Abbey); **The Playboy of the Western World** (Liverpool Playhouse); **A Quiet Life** and **Down the Line** (Peacock); **Buddleia** (Passion Machine/Dublin Theatre Festival/Donmar Warehouse). Film and TV credits include: **Family** by Roddy Doyle; **Plotlands; Soft Sand Blue Sea; Sunburn; The Claim; Watchmen** and **Lipservice.**

MARIE BREEN PRODUCTION MANAGER

Marie has previously worked with Rough Magic on **Olga, Shiver, Copenhagen, Dead Funny, Pentecost, The Whisperers** and **The School for Scandal**. Other recent work includes: **The Drunkard** (B*spoke); **Mermaids** (CoisCéim); Dublin Theatre Festival 2003 and 2002; the first International Dance Festival 2002; **The Book of Evidence** (Kilkenny Arts Festival/Fiach MacConghail); **My Brilliant Divorce** (Druid); **The Silver Tassie, The Flying Dutchman, Lady Macbeth of Mtsensk** and **Madama Butterfly** (Opera Ireland); **L'Altro Mondo** (Opera Machine); **Bread and Circus, Peeling Venus** and **The Salt Cycle** (Rex Levitates); **Macbeth, Romeo and Juliet** and **King Lear** (Second Age).

BREEGE BRENNAN PROPS BUYER

Breege has previously worked for Rough Magic as Administrator on **Midden**. Originally from Sligo, she has worked in professional theatre for 15 years. Other theatre credits include **Starlight Express** (West End, London) and productions with several Irish companies including The Gate, Fishamble and the Abbey. She has toured nationally and internationally with productions including **The Beckett Festival** (the Gate/Barbican and New Ambassadors, London) and **Pride and Prejudice** (the Gate/Spoleto Festival, Charleston, USA).

JOHN COMISKEY LIGHTING DESIGNER

John has previously worked with Rough Magic as Set and Lighting Designer on **Shiver** and **Copenhagen** (for which he won Best Designer in the 2002 Irish Times/ESB Irish Theatre Awards), and as Lighting Designer on **Three Days of Rain, Pentecost, The Way of the World, Love and a Bottle** and **The Country Wife**. Other lighting designs include productions for the Abbey, Druid, Daghdha, Siamsa Tíre, Project, and the dance/jewellery installation, **Lifecycles**, at the Crafts Council. Recent credits include Set and Lighting Designer on **Mermaids** (CoisCéim) and he co-designed the set and lighting for **The Shape of Metal** (Abbey) with Alan Farquharson.

John co-devised and directed **The Well** at the Dublin Theatre Festival 2000 and Gavin Friday's **Ich Liebe Dich**, to the music of Kurt Weill, at the Dublin Theatre Festival 2001. John was Production Director with **Riverdance: The Show** for two years, and was Artistic Director of Operating Theatre (with Roger Doyle) from 1984-1989. During this period he also collaborated with James Coleman as Lighting Designer on **Ignotum per Ignotius**, at the Douglas Hyde Gallery, and as Lighting and Video Designer on the installation/performance **Guaire: an Allegory in Dunguaire**, Kinvara.

He directed **Hit and Run**, Ireland's first dance film, which won the main prizes at the Toronto Moving Pictures and New York Dance On Screen festivals. John has also directed and produced documentaries on the **Dingle Wrens' Day** and the **Berlin Years of Agnes Bernelle**. He was a director with RTÉ for 12 years, during which time he directed hundreds of television programmes and created the visual style of numerous TV series including **Nighthawks, The Blackbird and The Bell** and **PopScene**. In 1995, he directed the **Eurovision Song Contest**.

ALAN FARQUHARSON SET DESIGNER

This is Alan's first production with Rough Magic. Other theatre designs include: **West Side Story, A Life, Bugsy Malone** and **Rent** (Olympia); **Borstal Boy** and **Sinbad** (Gaiety) and **An Solas Dearg** (Peacock). He recently co-designed the set and lighting for **The Shape of Metal** (Abbey) with John Comiskey. He joined the RTÉ Design Department in 1978 where he designed for **The Late Late Show, Kenny Live, Prime Time**, RTÉ News presentations and various outside broadcasts. He has worked as Production Designer on many of RTÉ's major film productions including **Dear Sarah, Diary of a Madman, The Truth About Clare, Hello Stranger** and **The Treaty**. He was also responsible for the Production Design of the **Eurovision Song Contest** in 1993 and 1995 and **Gael Force** (Point Theatre). Since leaving RTÉ as Senior Production Designer in August 1996 he has been responsible for the design of **Night Train** (Subotica Productions); **A Love Divided** (Parallel Films in association with RTÉ); **The Irish Tenors** (RDS/Waterfront, Belfast for Radius Television/PBS); **Relative Strangers** (Littlebird/Tatfilm); **A Secret Affair** (CBS/Adelson Entertainment/Metropolitan Films) and **The Nobel Peace Prize Concert** 1999 and 2000 (NRK Television).

Alan studied at the National College of Art & Design and now lectures in Production Design and Computer Aided Design at Dun Laoghaire Institute of Art, Design & Technology and has served on the council of The Institute of Designers in Ireland.

AISLING MOONEY STAGE DIRECTOR

This is Aisling's first production for Rough Magic. Other stage management credits include: **Cinderella, Hamelin, The Magic Flute, Erismena, Ariodante, The Love Potion** and **The Marriage of Figaro** (Opera Theatre Company); **Sive** (Druid); **The Drunkard** (B*spoke Theatre Company); **For the First Time Ever** (Pan Pan) and recently **Skylight** (Landmark Productions). Aisling studied stage management/production at Inchichore VEC for two years.

JUSTIN MURPHY STAGE MANAGER

This is Justin's first production with Rough Magic. He previously worked on **IL Giuramento** and **Sapho** (Wexford Festival Opera), **La Belle Helene** and **The Marriage of Figaro** (Castleward Opera) and **Our Country's Good** and **The Madras House** (BADA, London). He has also worked as a facilitator for Young Barecheek Drama School, Wexford and Bui Bolg Street Theatre.

EIMER Ní MHAOLDOMHNAIGH COSTUME DESIGNER

This is Eimer's first production with Rough Magic. Other theatre costume design credits include: **Made in China** (Peacock); **Please Don't Make Me Feel So Happy** (Olympia); and **Translations** (Hands Turn). Eimer's numerous film and television costume design credits include: **In America; Proof, Timbuktu; The Most Fertile Man in Ireland; Rebel Heart; About Adam; The Ambassador; The Castle; Gold in the Streets** and most recently, **Omagh** for Channel 4.

PAULA TIERNEY STAGE DIRECTOR

Paula's previous productions with Rough Magic include **Olga, Shiver, Copenhagen, Pentecost, Northern Star, Danti Dan, Hidden Charges, The Dogs** and **Digging for Fire**. Paula is a graduate of UCC and has spent ten years as a stage manager/operator on productions for Fishamble, Second Age, Bickerstaffe, Barabbas, Galloglass, Calypso, Red Kettle, the Everyman, the Gate and the Peacock. She has toured nationally and internationally with Opera Theatre Company, including **Zaide** (Antwerp), **The Magic Flute, Cosi Fan Tutte, The Marriage of Figaro, La Vera Constanza** and **Amadigi** (Melbourne Festival/BAM, New York/Lisbon/Porto/Paris). She has been Stage Director for both the Covent Garden and Buxton opera festivals and in Dublin for Opera Ireland on **Die Fledermaus, La Traviata, Boris Godunov** and **Aïda.** Other recent productions include: **Macbeth** (Second Age); **The Quest of the Good People** (Pavilion); **Kvetch** (Kilkenny Arts Festival); **Mermaids** (CoisCéim) and **Wexford Festival Opera**.

ROUGH MAGIC PRODUCTIONS

2003
OLGA by Laura Ruohonen in a new version by Linda McLean - IP

SHIVER by Declan Hughes - WP

2002
SCAN (international play-readings)
SEEDS new writing initiative, in association with the Dublin Fringe Festival.

COPENHAGEN by Michael Frayn - IP

2001
MIDDEN by Morna Regan - WP
DEAD FUNNY by Terry Johnson - IP

PLAYS[4] (international play-readings)

2000
THREE DAYS OF RAIN by Richard Greenberg - IP

PLAYS[4] (international play-readings)
PENTECOST by Stewart Parker - USP

1999
THE WHISPERERS Francis Sheridan's 'A Trip to Bath' as completed by Elizabeth Kuti - WP

BOOMTOWN by Pom Boyd, Declan Hughes and Arthur Riordan - WP

1998
THE SCHOOL FOR SCANDAL by Richard Brinsley Sheridan

1997
HALLOWEEN NIGHT by Declan Hughes - WP

MRS. SWEENEY by Paula Meehan - WP

1996
PENTECOST by Stewart Parker

NORTHERN STAR by Stewart Parker

1995
DANTI-DAN by Gina Moxley - WP

PENTECOST by Stewart Parker

1994
LADY WINDERMERE'S FAN by Oscar Wilde
DOWN ONTO BLUE by Pom Boyd - WP

HIDDEN CHARGES by Arthur Riordan - WP

1993
NEW MORNING by Declan Hughes - WP

THE WAY OF THE WORLD by William Congreve

1992
DIGGING FOR FIRE by Declan Hughes - UKP
BAT THE FATHER RABBIT THE SON by Donal O'Kelly
LOVE AND A BOTTLE by George Farquhar, adapted by Declan Hughes

THE DOGS by Donal O'Kelly - WP
THE EMERGENCY SESSION by Arthur Riordan - WP

1991

LOVE AND A BOTTLE by George Farquhar,
adapted by Declan Hughes - WP
LADY WINDERMERE'S FAN by Oscar Wilde

I CAN'T GET STARTED
by Declan Hughes - USP
DIGGING FOR FIRE by Declan Hughes - WP

1990

LADY WINDERMERE'S FAN by Oscar Wilde
I CAN'T GET STARTED
by Declan Hughes - WP

BAT THE FATHER RABBIT THE SON
by Donal O'Kelly

1989

BAT THE FATHER RABBIT THE SON
by Donal O'Kelly - UKP
A HANDFUL OF STARS by Billy Roche - IP

SPOKESONG by Stewart Parker
OUR COUNTRY'S GOOD
by Timberlake Wertenbaker - IP

1988

THE WHITE DEVIL by John Webster - IP
TOM AND VIV by Michael Hastings - IP
TEA AND SEX AND SHAKESPEARE
a new version by Thomas Kilroy

BAT THE FATHER RABBIT THE SON
by Donal O'Kelly - WP
SERIOUS MONEY by Caryl Churchill - IP

1987

NIGHTSHADE by Stewart Parker
ROAD by Jim Cartwright - IP
THE TEMPEST by Shakespeare
THE SILVER TASSIE by Sean O'Casey

A MUG'S GAME adaptation by the
company of Le Bourgeois Gentilhomme
and Everyman - IP

1986

MIDNITE AT THE STARLITE
by Michael Hastings
CAUCASIAN CHALK CIRCLE
by Bertolt Brecht
BETRAYAL by Harold Pinter - IP
**DOGG'S HAMLET, CAHOOT'S
MACBETH** by Tom Stoppard

DECADENCE by Steven Berkoff
AUNT DAN AND LEMON
by Wallace Shawn - IP
BLOODY POETRY by Howard Brenton
THE COUNTRY WIFE by William Wycherly
THE WOMAN IN WHITE adapted by Declan
Hughes from Wilkie Collins's novel - IP

1985

TOP GIRLS by Caryl Churchill
SEXUAL PERVERSITY IN CHICAGO
by David Mamet
VICTORY by Howard Barker - IP
NO END OF BLAME by Howard Barker - IP

THE ONLY JEALOUSY OF EMER by WB Yeats
MIDNITE AT THE STARLITE
by Michael Hastings - IP
CAUCASIAN CHALK CIRCLE
by Bertolt Brecht

1984

TALBOT'S BOX by Thomas Kilroy
FANSHEN by David Hare - IP
THE BIG HOUSE by Brendan Behan
THIRST by Myles na gCopaleen
DECADENCE by Steven Berkoff - IP

SEXUAL PERVERSITY IN CHICAGO
by David Mamet
TOP GIRLS by Caryl Churchill - IP
AMERICAN BUFFALO by David Mamet

WP = World première
IP = Irish première

UKP = UK première
USP = American première

FOR ROUGH MAGIC

ARTISTIC DIRECTOR **LYNNE PARKER**

EXECUTIVE PRODUCER **LOUGHLIN DEEGAN**

ADMINISTRATOR **ELIZABETH WHYTE**

BOARD OF DIRECTORS:

MARK MORTELL (CHAIR)

PAUL BRADY

MARIE BREEN

DARRAGH KELLY

JOHN McGOLDRICK

DERMOT McLAUGHLIN

PAULINE McLYNN

JOHN O'DONNELL

ADVISORY COUNCIL:

SIOBHÁN BOURKE

ANNE BYRNE

CATHERINE DONNELLY

DECLAN HUGHES

DARRAGH KELLY

PAULINE McLYNN

HÉLÈNE MONTAGUE

MARTIN MURPHY

ARTHUR RIORDAN

STANLEY TOWNSEND

ROUGH MAGIC THEATRE COMPANY

5/6 South Great Georges Street, Dublin 2, Ireland
T: + 353 1 6719278 **F:** + 353 1 6719301
E: info@rough-magic.com **W:** www.rough-magic.com
Registered number: 122753

Rough Magic gratefully acknowledges the support of the Arts
Council of Ireland, Dublin City Council and our Patrons.

TAKE ME AWAY

Gerald Murphy

To Orla

Characters

BREN, *mid thirties*

ANDY, *late twenties/early thirties*

KEV, *early twenties*

EDDIE, *mid fifties*

Set

Set in the front room of Bren's house. A clean space, carpet on the floor, with new furniture, a computer and a phone with an answering machine attached. Two doors, one to kitchen and bathroom, one to hall and rest of house.

Time

Contemporary Dublin. A sunny morning in early summer.

Ambience

The room should feel confined. The windows are shut throughout. The doors should be as if they are spring-loaded, i.e. they close automatically and any escape of 'atmosphere' from the room, as a door is opened, should be quickly closed off thereby emphasising this 'confinement'.

A slash (/) in the text indicates the point of interruption by the following speaker.

Scene One

Lights up. Morning. BREN *has his computer on and is sitting watching and clicking between images. He has just come in from work and is now at leisure. He is dressed in his uniform shirt with a jacket/sweater on a chair near him. There is a roll of toilet paper beside him.*

The doorbell rings.

BREN *stops. The doorbell rings again. Pause.* BREN *exits, creeping out to check who it is. The door shuts behind him. The doorbell keeps ringing.* BREN *returns. The door shuts behind him. The doorbell is replaced by knocking accompanied by* ANDY's *calling for him.*

ANDY (*off*). Bren? . . . It's Andy? Are you there, Bren?

    BREN *does not stir.*

    (*Off.*) . . . Bren? . . . Hello?

Pause. It seems as if ANDY *has gone away. Pause.* BREN *is drawn back to the computer. Lights down.*

Scene Two

Lights up. Late morning. The phone is ringing. The room is cleared (but for the toilet roll) with the computer turned off. The phone goes on to message.

BREN (*on answering machine*). Hello. Leave a message. Thanks.

ANDY (*on answering machine*). Ah shit.

    ANDY *does not continue with a message. Pause. The phone rings again.* BREN *enters from the bedroom. He is dressed in a bathrobe over pyjamas and a pair of slippers. He lets the phone go on to message.*

BREN (*on answering machine*). Hello. Leave a message. Thanks.

ANDY (*on answering machine*). Yeah Bren – it's Andy – yeah – I don't have much credit but yeah anyway I was at your door this morning – don't know if you heard me cos I knocked – I'm outside now – cos I was hoping to catch you cos we're all leaving from your gaf – I don't know but anyway I'll hang on a bit I suppose – no but cos we're all going over to Ma in the hospital leaving from your gaf – that's why I called over – shit – is there no power left – is that gone now – hello? – shit!

Pause. BREN rewinds the tape and plays it again. As the tape begins ANDY hears it and knocks on the door and presses the doorbell. BREN has been caught out.

ANDY (*off*). Bren? It's me – Andy. . . . Bren, are you there?

BREN keeps the tape playing and waits to hear it out. He rewinds the tape – straightens up and is about to answer the door but spots the toilet roll. He exits with the toilet roll to the bathroom. The door shuts behind him.

Bren? It's Andy . . . Hello? . . . Bren?

BREN enters (the door shuts behind him), straightens up and exits to answer the door to ANDY. The door shuts behind him.

BREN and ANDY enter. The door shuts behind them.

ANDY has a cut/hardened blood on his forehead. He is dressed in dirty jeans, trainers and a T-shirt.

Did you not hear me at the door?

BREN. What's going on?

ANDY. I should've phoned you first – I just didn't think of it this morning.

BREN. What happened your head?

ANDY. Is that *your* computer?

BREN. You're calling over here – what d'you mean – 'going over to see Ma'?

ANDY. Did you not get the message?

BREN. Ma's in hospital?

ANDY. Did the oul fella not ring you?

BREN. No.

ANDY. So you don't know then?

BREN. Know what?

ANDY. Ma's sick – we're all going over to visit her – leaving from here at four o'clock.

BREN. . . . What?

ANDY. Yeah he didn't say what was wrong with her but – he was half-jarred – you know yourself? So what do you use it (*the computer*) for? Is it new?

BREN. . . . Were you drinking this morning?

ANDY. What?

BREN. You were at an early house – were you?

ANDY. I was not at an early house.

BREN. . . . I was asleep.

ANDY. That's why I was over early but you must've gone straight to bed when you came home – did you?

BREN. What's? – What do you mean 'we're all going over' – what – who's 'we'?

ANDY. Us – the oul fella – Kev – you know – a family visit kind of thing – see how she is – what's up with her – well I kind of have a fair idea anyway.

BREN. Does that – Deirdre and Gordon – are they coming as well?

ANDY. She's not sure – she'll try but.

BREN. Leaving at four o'clock?

ANDY. Yeah.

BREN. But sure you're five hours early.

ANDY. It's a bit stuffy in here Bren – would you not open a window or something?

BREN. . . . You're in another dispute – is that it – you and Deirdre?

ANDY. What? What dispute? What're you talking about?

BREN. I don't want to have to deal with another dispute – if she's coming over here – I don't want that – this is my house – all right?

ANDY. I'm here cos of the pram shop Bren – the – down the road there – Deirdre sent me – okay? That's why I'm early.

BREN. Nobody said anything to me about this.

ANDY. That's the oul fella for you.

BREN. But sure I've to sleep.

ANDY. We're all on nights Bren – you know? But this is a family thing – he wants us all together.

BREN. . . . What happened your head?

ANDY. . . . Would you notice it?

BREN. Why d'you think I'm asking you?

ANDY. Bloody junkies – hurlies they had.

BREN. Junkies with hurlies?

ANDY. Half seven this morning – I couldn't believe it.

BREN. Junkies with hurlies at half seven in the morning?

ANDY. Four or five of them – I only just got paid – cleaned me out they did.

BREN. Cleaned you out?

ANDY. It's what this country's coming to – it's a disgrace – law and order and all that – nasty looking – is it?

BREN. . . . I don't have any money – all right?

ANDY (*pause*). Take that back Bren!

BREN (*pause*). I was asleep . . . this is the first I've heard of this.

ANDY. I'll go down and show you where it happened – if you don't believe me.

BREN. . . . They hit you over the head with hurlies?

ANDY. It all happened very quick like – they turned on me and the next minute they're gone.

BREN. . . . You're checking out a pram? So does that mean you're going away and coming back – is that it?

ANDY. Well that's it – we're all going away – that's why we're coming here – this is the meeting point.

BREN. . . . This is my house.

ANDY. . . . No you see what I'd say it is – is that home's a kip since Ma was taken in and he doesn't want us to see that so that's why we're here – either that or we're nearer the hospital.

BREN. . . . What hospital is she in?

ANDY. James's.

BREN. Sure I'm not near James's!

ANDY. No but we're nearer James's than home would be.

BREN. . . . And – and he didn't tell you what was wrong with Ma – no?

ANDY. No but you know yourself – us all going over to see her like . . .

BREN. . . . What?

ANDY. Well like – I mean – she's had this chest infection – it's – for a long time now.

BREN. She never said anything to me about it.

ANDY. . . . Do you be talking to Ma?

BREN. . . . An odd time – she rings me up – never said anything about a chest infection.

ANDY. Well no, her chest's been bad now for ages Bren – you know – Deirdre told me.

BREN. Is Deirdre coming over here or not – or what?

ANDY. . . . Well – you know – she's not sure – she might.

BREN. Well will you ring her and find out?

ANDY. Yeah. Ah yeah.

BREN. Go on then . . .

ANDY. No you see she's out shopping now and she doesn't have a mobile.

BREN. But – why aren't you in your own house?

ANDY. Because – I told you – she wants me to price a buggy.

BREN. Well go on then – price the buggy.

ANDY. No see I have to ring her first cos she has a particular make in mind. I forgot – it's been a bit of a hectic morning.

BREN. . . . I've to work tonight.

ANDY. Sure don't we all?

BREN. . . . But why *my* house – why not yours – even?

ANDY. Ring the oul fella – ask him?

BREN. . . . You think it's a chest infection – is that it?

ANDY. Yeah well a serious chest infection and then what it leads on to – more so . . .

BREN. What d'you mean – 'leads on to'?

ANDY. Well we've all been asked to see her so like it's not a cough she has – she's hospitalised.

BREN. . . . She tells me everything – it's not something she wouldn't tell me about.

ANDY. Well we'll find out when the oul fella gets here and then we'll see who's right.

BREN. I don't care who's right – why are yis meeting here?

ANDY. . . . Were you at Mrs C's funeral?

BREN. No why, were you?

ANDY. No, I couldn't make it.

BREN. . . . So, what about it?

ANDY. Yeah well you know, Ma was her only friend in the
    world Bren – twenty-five years she was calling over there –
    looking after her.

BREN. . . . So?

ANDY. . . . It doesn't matter – go on to bed – I won't disturb
    you.

BREN. . . . What're you talking about?

ANDY. We'll find out when the oul fella gets here – all right?

BREN. Find out what?

ANDY. I'm just saying that just – you're always better off
    thinking the worst in these situations – cos at least then
    everything's never as bad as you thought it would be –
    every cloud has a silver lining and all that – that's all I'm
    saying.

BREN. . . . What?

ANDY. Mrs C. – the funeral . . . it doesn't matter.

BREN. Ring Deirdre – will you?

ANDY. She's out shopping Bren – it takes a long time when
    you've a kid – you know?

    The doorbell rings. BREN *freezes.*

    Now I bet you that's Kev.

    BREN *does not stir. Pause. The doorbell rings again.*

    Do you want me to get it?

    BREN *answers* ANDY *with a look and exits. The door
    shuts behind him.*

BREN *and* KEV *enter. The door shuts behind them.* KEV *is dressed casual/trendy.*

BREN. I wasn't even told Ma was sick. Is that what you're here for?

KEV. Yeah he said to come over here – to visit her.

ANDY (*to* KEV). How're you Kev – are you still wetting the bed?

KEV. What?

ANDY. Just off the Galway train, are you?

KEV. What happened your head?

ANDY. Would you believe it – coming out of work this morning – junkies, took my wages they did.

KEV. Jesus – are you all right?

ANDY. Ah sure, I'll live – won't I – what?

BREN (*to* KEV). At half seven this morning?

ANDY. He (*indicates* BREN) doesn't believe me. But you'd imagine he'd be used to seeing that sort of thing – wouldn't you?

BREN. Why's that?

ANDY. Well you're in security – aren't you?

BREN. It's not that kind of security.

ANDY. How're you keeping Kev anyway?

KEV. Grand – yeah.

BREN. You're very early.

KEV. Yeah I didn't want to be late – so I left early just in case I would be late – so I wasn't – late.

ANDY (*to* KEV). What d'you think of his computer?

KEV. Is that yours?

ANDY. What do you use it for?

BREN. Work.

ANDY. You're working from home now?

BREN (*to* KEV). Da told you to come straight here – did he?

ANDY (*to* BREN). Was it the promotion got you that?

BREN. For four o'clock?

KEV. Oh yeah congratulations – Mam told me.

ANDY (*to* BREN). I don't know how you do that sitting in front of a screen all night – looking at car parks – it must be very boring – is it?

BREN. Sorry?

ANDY. How much is your mortgage Bren, if you don't mind me asking? I'll tell you how much my rent is.

BREN. I don't care about your rent.

ANDY. No I'm just saying fair play to you – you got the money together.

KEV (*to* BREN). Is it a two-bedroomed?

ANDY. All you need now is a nice little wife. Do you have a nice little wife locked away upstairs – no?

BREN. Are you finished – I'm trying to talk to him?

ANDY. Don't mind me Bren.

BREN (*to* KEV). . . . You were talking to Da – Kev – were you?

KEV. Yeah see I ring in every week to keep in touch.

BREN. And what – what hospital did he say she was in?

KEV. I don't know . . . was it the Mater?

BREN. The Mater? Are you sure?

KEV. Well I think – well it could've been Beaumont – I don't know.

BREN. Beaumont? Sure I'd never get over and back to Beaumont – not with the traffic at four o'clock.

ANDY. Well if you don't want to go Bren – I'm sure Ma'd understand.

BREN. Well how are you going to get to work?

ANDY. Well as far as I know it's James's.

BREN (*to* KEV). Are you sure it wasn't James's he said – no?

KEV. Yeah – I don't know – maybe I just thought it was the Mater cos that's the hospital I think of when I think of hospitals and you asked me.

BREN. But he didn't say James's?

KEV. Well he was a bit pissed I think so he was going on about what was wrong with Mam – more so – than the hospital.

ANDY. He told you what was wrong with her?

KEV. Yeah he just said it's something all women go through.

ANDY. What is?

KEV. The 'menopause'.

ANDY. . . . No – sure – she had that already Kev.

KEV. . . . Yeah – no – I think that – he said it's a relapse.

ANDY. A 'relapse'? No sure she got all the works out the last time.

KEV. Yeah but he said that her tubes were rotted and that she got them cut out or that she'd have to get more of them cut out or that they grew back or something.

ANDY. No – no Kev – she got *all* the works out the last time, the tubes, the eggs, the whole lot – do you not remember?

KEV. . . . . Yeah, I don't know. It's her womb then or something.

ANDY. You don't really know much about the female body Kev – do you?

KEV. Well – well – that's just what he said to me – I'm just . . .

ANDY. They took her womb out as well – it saves them having to go back in a second time – that's what they do.

KEV. Right well anyway, as long as it's not anything serious –
that's the main thing – isn't it – that's what he said.

ANDY. I didn't say it wasn't anything serious.

BREN (*to* ANDY). You haven't a clue what you're talking
about. Ma had a hysterectomy – do you know what that is?

ANDY. What? I was at my own son's birth – Bren – so – you
know, I think I do know a thing or two – all right?

BREN. But you don't know what a hysterectomy is though –
do you?

ANDY. What? How many girlfriends have you had Bren?

BREN. Sorry?

ANDY (*to* BREN). What? Look all I'm saying is I have a kid
so I do know a thing or two – all right?

BREN. You could've fooled me.

ANDY. What's that supposed to mean?

BREN. Ring Deirdre – will you do that?

ANDY. . . . Deirdre's at the clinic Bren – I told you.

BREN. Shopping, you said.

ANDY. Yeah and the clinic.

KEV. Is she sick?

ANDY. No – Gordon – it's a check-up for Gordon.

KEV. Why is he not well?

ANDY. Yeah he is well – it's just a check-up.

KEV. Oh right. And how's Deirdre?

ANDY. What? She's grand. How are you?

KEV. Yeah grand.

ANDY. What're you working at again?

KEV. Programming.

ANDY. Yeah – like what?

KEV. What do you mean?

ANDY. Programming? What kind of programming?

KEV. Computer programming.

ANDY. Yeah cos I tried to ring you once but I couldn't get the number.

KEV. . . . That's cos it's an American company – the number's not available to the public – it's only business.

BREN. And you don't work nights at all?

KEV. No.

ANDY. So you're on a bigger salary than him (*indicates* BREN) – then are you?

BREN. Don't mind him.

ANDY. You're a big shot?

KEV. No.

ANDY. How long are you out of college now – six months – is it?

KEV. Five.

ANDY. Five – right, so – well – so tell me this Kev – how was Ma's chest infection then – when you were there?

KEV. Did she have a chest infection?

BREN (*to* ANDY). Now – you see – what did I say to you?

ANDY (*to* KEV). Were you at Mrs C's funeral – Ma's friend?

KEV. . . . Yeah, I was, yeah.

BREN. Your work let you take time off – did they?

KEV. Yeah – they did.

ANDY. What was it like?

KEV. It was – the church and then we went over to the cemetery and we went to a pub then.

ANDY. Was it a big do, a small do? What was the coffin made of?

KEV. . . . Wood?

ANDY. Was there many people there?

KEV. No.

BREN. And how did Ma take it?

KEV. I think like – she kind of cried a bit – well she did – a bit.

BREN. I meant to go myself but I can't just get off work like that – was Ma asking for me?

KEV. No. She kind of had a friend there, Jess, she was with her most of the time – she didn't really talk to me.

BREN. Was Da not there – no?

KEV. No.

ANDY. This – her friend – she's not another – Mrs C. job – Ma's not looking after her – like she goes to the toilet and everything?

KEV. Yeah I'd say so – she stands up and everything – she's tall.

ANDY. Put me down if I ever lose control – will you do that for me – put me down?

BREN. Is this the woman that works in the home?

KEV. Yeah – I don't know – I think so.

ANDY. But there was no family belonging to Mrs C. there?

KEV. No I don't think she had any family.

ANDY. No she didn't and Ma was her only friend – twenty-five years changing her nappy.

KEV. Right.

ANDY. Well that's not true cos she had a budgie and he was her friend but he dropped dead one day. You see Bren was always feeding him . . .

BREN. Don't mind him.

ANDY. So Ma's chest was acting up at the funeral I'd say – was it?

BREN. Give over – will you?

ANDY. What? Ma's in hospital – what do *you* think it is?

BREN. I don't know – and we won't know until Da gets here – all right?

KEV. Well Da said it was 'menopause' . . .

ANDY. He's only saying that cos he doesn't know what to say and he's not going to say it on the phone anyway – and anyway he's in a state of shock – I mean – sure he can't even boil an egg without help – his soft boiled egg – sure he's had a full-time housewife since he got married.

KEV. He's just into himself really – I think.

ANDY. Is that what *you* think?

KEV. Well I mean he doesn't say very much he just – comes in – in the morning and goes into the boxroom and sticks on his headphones – doesn't he?

ANDY (*sings*). 'But most of all you're my best friend.'

BREN. Shut up will you?

KEV. Yeah.

ANDY (*sings*). 'You're my *egg* – / when I'm hungry.'

BREN. Shut up!

ANDY (*to* KEV). You see when you're my age – you know what that song's about.

BREN. You're not in the pub now – / Andy – all right?

ANDY. You see cos not only is she everything but she's your friend as well – like she's not shouting at you – she's buying you a pint.

KEV. Right.

ANDY. You haven't a clue Kev – have you?

BREN. Leave him alone.

ANDY (*to* KEV). So the oul fella wasn't verbally abusing you then – he verbally abused me the whole time, that I was a waster and all that.

BREN (*to* ANDY). Are you gonna continue with this – are you?

ANDY. I'm just telling him so he knows.

BREN. Do you need to know?

KEV. I don't know.

ANDY. When are we gonna start paying him back so's he can retire – this is when I was ten years of age.

BREN. He never said that to me.

ANDY. Well I must've been picked out for the special treatment.

BREN (*to* ANDY). Right – yeah.

ANDY (*to* KEV). You see you were spoilt cos you were an accident – I was planned – he (*indicates* BREN) was a 'love child'.

BREN. How many pints did you have this morning?

ANDY (*to* KEV). Sure we weren't allowed pets but you got a guinea pig – two days it lasted – guess who killed it?

BREN. Don't mind him.

ANDY. You (*to* KEV) pissed the bed one morning – Ma lost the head – he decides to teach you a lesson.

BREN. The dog next door put it into his mouth.

ANDY. I saw you taking him out and playing football with him.

BREN (*to* KEV). He (*indicates* ANDY) was in the early house this morning . . .

KEV. I didn't even know I had a guinea pig.

ANDY. And he puts you up on the shed – bawling your eyes out – / you don't know what's going on.

BREN (*to* ANDY). Look are you ringing Deirdre?

ANDY. Puts the dead little guinea pig into your lap – 'now that'll teach you a lesson' he says.

BREN. Are you finished now?

ANDY. But you just kept on pissing anyway but that was all right cos the oul fella never bothered you about it he even got you a doctor and Ma never even clattered you either – did she?

KEV. You wet the bed as well.

ANDY. But did she clatter you?

KEV. She told me off loads of times.

ANDY. Ah well then you're made – aren't you? And I suppose Da told you off as well – did he?

KEV. Da just ignored me.

ANDY. He paid for your bed-wetting doctor and your college – didn't he?

BREN. Ring Deirdre – will you?

ANDY. That's not ignoring you Kev.

KEV. . . . . I mean saying 'hello' to me or anything – there was none of that.

ANDY. We never got a bed-wetting specialist come see us Kev.

BREN. Ring her – will you?

ANDY. Did you ever have to queue in a clinic Bren – did you?

BREN. What's your point?

ANDY. Young ones queuing out the door for free nappies and junkies hassling you for odds – / kids screaming at you.

BREN. So – she's not back then yet – is that it?

ANDY. No.

BREN. Right, well – will you just shut up?

ANDY. You go on to bed Bren – you're tired.

BREN. I'll go to bed when I want to go to bed – all right?

ANDY. Are you not tired?

BREN. Yeah I am tired. Tired of listening to you!

> BREN *gets up and walks towards the kitchen. To* KEV, *behind* BREN*'s back,* ANDY *mimics* BREN*'s last response.*

ANDY. Are you making tea?

BREN. No!

> BREN *enters the kitchen. The door shuts behind him.*

ANDY. . . . That's true about the guinea pig – you know that don't you?

KEV. I don't remember it.

ANDY. Yeah he kicked him up in the air a few times and smashed him off the wall . . . Ah there was loads of other things he did. I had a book once – I was really into it but then it just disappeared and I thought I lost it but then years later I found it – he had buried it over the next door neighbour's wall. A great book it was – Mrs C. gave it to me. Did you ever meet her – Mrs C.?

KEV. Yeah I did – once or twice.

ANDY. Smelly – wasn't she?

KEV. . . . Yeah.

ANDY. That smell – that was from her nappies.

KEV. Right.

ANDY. You see I had loads of interests when I was kid and I used to read but I never got encouraged in my reading – d'you know what I mean? But she gave me a book – Mrs C. – you see she was into animals – so she gave me this book about this young lad and his sheep dog – / in the snow on a farm.

BREN *enters. The door shuts behind him. He has a 'milk moustache'.*

BREN. I'm going to go to bed – all right? So keep your / voices down.

ANDY. Was that milk you had?

BREN. What?

ANDY. Your lip.

BREN. Oh right.

BREN *wipes his mouth clean with a tissue from his robe pocket.*

ANDY. I wouldn't mind a glass of milk for the heartburn – you know?

BREN. I've only a sup left and I need it for my cup of tea.

ANDY. . . . Right. Go on then. Go on to bed.

BREN. . . . Just keep the noise down.

ANDY. Yeah I will . . . Go on – I'm telling him something.

BREN. And don't be touching anything.

ANDY. I won't touch your computer Bren – I swear – go on to bed.

BREN. . . . No I wouldn't sleep now anyway.

ANDY. The pressure of the promotion getting to you – is it?

BREN *sits down.*

BREN. . . . I'll doze off here if you keep it quiet – all right?

ANDY. Right . . . fair enough.

Pause. BREN *sitting – eyes open –* ANDY *waiting on him to doze. Pause.*

Right – go on then – doze.

BREN. I'll doze when I want to doze.

ANDY. . . . Right – go on then.

BREN (*pause*). Just keep it quiet.

BREN shuts his eyes. Pause.

KEV. Before you doze off Bren – could I have a shower?
Would you mind? It was just I was up very early this
morning and I didn't have time.

BREN opens his eyes.

BREN. The water hasn't come on yet.

KEV. Oh right.

BREN. . . . You'll live will you?

KEV. Yeah – I suppose.

BREN. Right.

*Pause. BREN shuts his eyes. Pause. ANDY and KEV lower
their voices.*

ANDY. So anyway one of the sheep goes missing and the boy
goes off and the snow's really coming down but then he
finds her. And she's stuck in a ditch looking up at him –
baaing away – shivering. So he digs around and he gets her
free but doesn't he fall down into the ditch himself. But he
has a dog with him – did I say that?

KEV. Yeah.

ANDY. Yeah well the dog sees he's trapped and he goes off to
get the master but it looks like the little boy is going to
freeze to death but then this nice old farmer fella comes
along and rescues him – a nice old fella – nothing dirty
about him – do you know what I mean? And the little boy
really likes him but then when the master and his missus
come along the farmer fella's gone – he just vanishes – no
footprints or anything and the boy tries to explain to his
folks but they don't listen to him – and the Da takes out a
bottle of brandy – and the mother says . . . 'Is it all right for
him to be drinking brandy?' and the father says – 'Yes it's
fine just so long as he doesn't develop a taste for it.' And the
little boy takes a sup but he spits it out straight away and
everybody laughs . . . I loved that story.

KEV. . . . Yeah.

ANDY. What do you mean – 'yeah'? What do you know?

KEV. What? I don't know.

ANDY. That book was buried – I found it.

KEV. Right.

ANDY. . . . How much are you on a week Kev?

KEV. . . . That's – mind your own business.

ANDY. I'm not going to tell anyone.

KEV. I'm not telling you.

ANDY. I'm just curious. I mean we could have a millionaire for a brother and we wouldn't know.

KEV. I'm not a millionaire.

ANDY. How did you get that job?

KEV. They came round to the college recruiting people.

ANDY. But sure didn't you fail your first year?

KEV. Yeah but that was just first year.

ANDY. You had to pay fees for that college – didn't you?

KEV. Yeah.

ANDY. So are you paying him back now then – the oul fella?

KEV. That's my business.

ANDY. So you're not then?

KEV. I'm not telling you.

ANDY. Jesus Kev – what's your problem? I'll tell you how much I make.

KEV. Why do you want to know?

ANDY. Cos – I just want to know.

KEV. Well I'm not telling you!

ANDY. . . . Kev, look – you were the last to leave – like did
you see anything? Bits of blood and phlegm down the toilet
or anything?

KEV. What?

ANDY. Ma – the chest infection?

KEV. No.

ANDY. Was she taking tablets?

KEV. . . . I think she took antibiotics.

ANDY. She was always on antibiotics Kev – come on – like –
was there anything strange – anything she might've done?

KEV (*pause*). Well, she – she bought a blouse once with a
picture of a beach on it and she said that she didn't know
why she bought it. I thought that was a bit strange.

ANDY. . . . Do you have a girlfriend Kev?

KEV. . . . What? Yeah I do yeah.

ANDY. And she's never bought anything that she didn't wear –
no?

KEV. I think she went to her doctor a lot.

ANDY. . . . Your man? Sure he felt me up – four years of age I
was – you know the way they feel your balls – that test?

KEV. I had a lady doctor.

ANDY. Oh you jammy bastard you.

KEV. Yeah and she gave me a lump of sugar.

ANDY. How did she give it to you?

KEV. What do you mean?

ANDY. Like were your kecks down and she kind of puts it into
your mouth – like that – ('*imitating*' *the doctor*) was it?

KEV. No.

ANDY. Did you get her number?

KEV. Yeah I would've but I wasn't able to write yet.

ANDY. You think that's funny – do you? Come on Kev – there must be something – come on!

KEV. I don't know.

ANDY. Ma is always going to the doctor's – like where would she be if she didn't have a pain to complain about Kev?

KEV. I don't know – ask Da!

Lights down.

Scene Three

Lights up. Early afternoon. BREN *is deep in sleep. There is an empty carton of milk beside* ANDY.

ANDY. . . . So do I know her then – this girlfriend?

KEV. . . . I wouldn't say so.

ANDY. . . . And she has a good job and all like yourself – yeah?

KEV. . . . Yeah.

ANDY. And you're not going out with anyone else – I suppose – are you?

KEV. What?

ANDY. No – no – Kev – no – no – bad move. Have the craic – you know? All those young ones out there in the nightclubs gagging for it – I'm telling you – cos when you reach my age that's it. You get up – you go to work – you come home. And no matter what you do then – it's never enough – like I mean what I'm earning – do you know what I mean? So what's the point?

KEV. . . . Right.

ANDY. . . . I mean like Deirdre – You see – she – she – she looks up to her brother too much – down the country –

in Limerick they are – with the house and a swing in the
garden and he throws the stick to the dog and all that – do
you know what I mean? But it's just money . . . Deirdre
used to work – you see – she used to live in London – she
has a friend over there but ever since she had Gordon –
I don't know – I love him – I mean – like I've a shit job so
that's what I'm saying – for him – for Gordon – to give him
a chance like – a proper set-up and all that – d'you know
what I mean? . . . The bit of money?

KEV. . . . Yeah.

ANDY. You haven't a clue Kev have you?

KEV. Yeah I think I do.

ANDY. I don't care if you do or not – all I'm saying is you're
young – so just keep it that way.

KEV. I don't think you're that old.

ANDY. Ah believe me Kev.

KEV. No – you see I think that – that you can always change
like – that there's always other ways of looking at things –
like – I mean – at the world – that – that it doesn't always
have to be the same – that – it's just your view and that
you're not always the kind of person people think you are –
that – that – that's true.

ANDY. . . . What're you talking about?

KEV. That – the way people see you and for forgiveness and
that – that you have to talk cos otherwise people don't
know what's going on in your head – you have to express
yourself – that's what it's about.

ANDY. You haven't a clue Kev – you know – like I mean when
you're working nights – like – it's the day – but like – you
have to sleep . . . You see I'm being bullied at work – the
boss, she's a woman – I'm not even welding anymore – I'm
just on the floor – don't tell anyone that – so like you're just
sitting there – the early house – the few pints but sure you
can't relax cos you're going over everything you want to
say – like – I want to tell the boss to screw herself – 'fuck

you and your poxy fucking job'– what d'you think of that?
How d'you think Deirdre'd react – if I walked out of me
job – what d'you think she'd say?

KEV. Yeah – I don't know.

ANDY. She would not be pleased Kev. No I mean I do love her
and everything at this stage . . . so that's why I'm asking you.

KEV. . . . What?

ANDY. The last time you were home – Ma? Everything was
normal – she went to the shops, she made your dinner, she
ironed your jocks – is that it?

KEV. She never ironed my jocks.

ANDY. Did she not?

KEV. No.

ANDY. She always gave mine a quick run over – that was with
the 'Y-fronts' – I mean she didn't do it when the other
things came in – the little panty things. Did you ever wear
them?

KEV. No it was all boxer shorts in my day.

ANDY. Ah yeah. He wore them anyway – panties – didn't
you? Bren? Panties? Panties?

BREN *stays sleeping.*

Amazing – isn't it? He just has to close his eyes. (*Pause.*)
What d'you think of his gaf?

KEV. Is it a two-bedroomed?

ANDY. Yeah – why?

KEV. I don't know.

ANDY. You see Bren just has himself to worry about – he
saves all his money – d'you know what I mean?

KEV. I think he's done pretty well for himself.

ANDY (*to* BREN). Panties. Panties – Bren – panties – panties
. . . (*To* KEV.) Are we getting each other Christmas presents

this year – do you think? They're deadly slippers (*indicates* BREN*'s slippers*) them, aren't they?

KEV. Yeah – no.

ANDY (*pause*). It's the big 'C' Kev.

KEV. What? What do you mean?

ANDY. Ma – it's the big 'C'.

KEV. What do you mean?

ANDY. Ma – she has cancer.

KEV. She has cancer?

ANDY. Yeah.

KEV. Jesus.

ANDY. . . . Yeah.

KEV. How do you know?

ANDY. Because she's gonna make an announcement about it. She wants us all there. She's been told how long she's left.

KEV. . . . Jesus.

ANDY. . . . Shocking – isn't it?

KEV. . . . She – she told you this?

ANDY. Well why else are we going over? Think about it? She's in hospital – she wants to see us all and with her chest – it's obvious.

KEV. . . . But she didn't actually tell you?

ANDY. Jesus Kev – cop on – will you – she's not going to just tell you!

KEV. But you don't know for definite you're just saying.

ANDY. It's cancer Kev but if you don't believe me then – you know – just wait till the oul fella gets here. I just thought you should know now anyway but it doesn't matter . . . Turn on his computer there – see if he wakes up – go on.

KEV. That's awful if she has cancer.

ANDY. Yeah well these things happen – just don't say anything to the oul fella about it cos Ma wants to tell us herself – that's what this is about – you know? . . . Anyway I want to just see what he's got on it – come on – for the craic.

KEV. What? No I don't want to do that.

ANDY. Did you ever get a hurley across the head Kev? D'you know the sort of pain I'm going through – do you?

KEV. He'll wake up. When it comes on there's a bit of music.

ANDY. Well can you turn that off?

KEV. Yeah but you have to turn it on first.

ANDY. . . . You know what he's watching on it – don't you? Sure he's an addict. Since he was in school. And he never had a girlfriend and there was all that shit with your woman – what's her name? Your mate's sister. Remember when the knickers went missing? Sure you got the blame for it.

KEV. Lorraine?

ANDY. Yeah – Lorraine. That was him (*indicates* BREN). Sure he used to take them off the clotheslines and then he took hers and you got branded then as the 'knicker thief'. And that girl went schizo after – didn't she? I mean what age was she – at the time?

KEV. Thirteen – I think.

ANDY. Yeah just starting to develop – and he was what?

KEV. About twenty-two – I suppose.

ANDY. Yeah about your age – you know? Like would you do something like that – steal some little schoolgirl's panties? Of course you wouldn't . . . And you're made out to be the pervert then. That must've been shit for you – was it? . . . Like do you not want to get your own back on him?

KEV. I don't know.

ANDY. And for the guinea pig as well?

KEV. . . . I think we all make mistakes.

ANDY. No – no – no – it's not that Kev. It's – look – Ma
thinks he's the business. Like with his promotion and his
house and all that but she hasn't a clue . . . That's why I
think we should find out if he's up to anything with this
yoke (*indicates computer*) . . . Like if he's getting into
pervy shit – I mean – we could help him – wouldn't you
like to do that for your brother – help him out?

KEV. It's just it'll make a lot of noise.

ANDY. Bren'd sleep through a blow job Kev – not that he's
ever going to get one – but d'you know what I mean?
(*To* BREN – *up close.*) Panties Bren – Lorraine's panties
Bren – panties. (BREN *does not stir. To* KEV.) See – like
a corpse . . . Go on . . . go on.

KEV *turns on the computer.* BREN *doesn't stir. The doorbell rings.* KEV *switches off the computer.* BREN *wakes.*

BREN. The phone – phone – phone – phone / don't answer it –
it's all right.

ANDY. It's the door.

BREN. What? You woke me up.

ANDY. It's the front door Bren.

BREN. Who's at the door?

ANDY. It's the oul fella – I'd say.

BREN. Oh right – right – the front door.

BREN *exits to answer the door. The door shuts behind him.*

ANDY. I'm just going to the jacks – all right?

KEV. Right.

ANDY *exits to the bathroom. The door shuts behind him.*

EDDIE *enters followed by* BREN. *The door shuts behind
them.* EDDIE *is a little dressed up, e.g. open-necked shirt
(badly ironed), trousers and with shoes shined.*

EDDIE (*entering*). Good. That's good. Right. Ah how're you
Kevin?

KEV. How're you Da?

EDDIE. How are you?

KEV. Yeah good and yourself?

EDDIE. Yeah good – yeah. This is a nice place you have here
    Brendan – very nice. Is it quiet?

BREN. Yeah it's quiet.

EDDIE. Yeah your mother said it was quiet.

BREN. Yeah it's quiet.

EDDIE. . . . Is it a bit stuffy – would you not open a window –
    it's a lovely day out there?

BREN. They're locked. See I'm asleep during the day – so
    there's no point in opening them.

EDDIE. Oh – right – well we're all here now anyway – that's
    the main thing . . . Where's Anthony?

KEV. He's in the jacks.

EDDIE. And Deirdre and Gordon?

BREN. Are they coming?

EDDIE. What d'you mean? Where are they?

BREN. I didn't know anything about this Da – I didn't even
    know *you* were coming.

EDDIE. What? I rang you – I left you a message. Where's
    Deirdre and Gordon?

BREN. . . . Ask Andy – he'll tell you.

EDDIE. They better be coming.

BREN. Why are they coming?

EDDIE. What? You – you got promoted I heard – did you?

BREN. Yeah.

EDDIE. So what's it you're doing now?

BREN. I'm in a control centre. So we're all – / leaving from
    here.

EDDIE. You have this place looking spick and span anyway.

BREN. Right. So what's happening then – / we're all leaving from here?

EDDIE. Are you on your own or have you a 'partner' – isn't that what they say these days – what?

BREN. No.

EDDIE. You're on your own then – are you?

BREN. So we're all leaving from here for the hospital – is that it?

EDDIE. What? I – will you let me – I'm not going to be explaining it all to you individually – all right?

BREN. Explaining what?

EDDIE. What did I just say?

BREN. Right – well I've to go to work Da so just to let you know.

EDDIE. And you – you Kevin – how are you?

KEV. Good – yeah, good.

EDDIE. The Galway job going well?

KEV. Yeah.

EDDIE. You got the train – did you?

KEV. Yeah I did. Is – So how's Ma?

EDDIE. What? – Is that a computer, Brendan?

BREN. Yeah.

EDDIE. What's it for?

BREN. It's – what – I use it for work.

EDDIE. Do you work from home now as well?

BREN. Yeah.

EDDIE. I wouldn't know how to turn the thing on myself.

BREN. So why are we leaving from my house?

EDDIE. Sorry?

BREN. Well – it's my house Da – you know like I wouldn't invite myself over to Kev's house – d'you know what I mean?

EDDIE. What? That's – this is the arrangement – that's what I said – 'leaving from here'.

BREN. Is it handier for the hospital – is that it?

EDDIE. What's keeping Anthony?

KEV. He must be having a bit of a clearout or something – I'd say.

EDDIE. What?

BREN. So which hospital is Ma in then – cos Kev thinks it's – what did you say? 'James's' – was it?

KEV. Or the Mater – I think – I'm not sure – either one or Beaumont?

BREN (*to* EDDIE). Is it James's or the Mater or Beaumont?

EDDIE. I'd like a cup of tea Brendan – if you don't mind.

BREN. Well I'd just like to know Da cos – you know – getting over and back in the traffic – it makes a difference.

EDDIE. Could you do that for me?

BREN. . . . You want tea?

EDDIE. Yeah – thanks for offering all the same – what?

Pause. BREN *gets up.*

KEV (*to* BREN). D'you want a hand?

BREN. Sorry?

KEV. To make the tea?

BREN. 'Do I want a hand?'

KEV. . . . Yeah.

EDDIE. He's joking. Aren't you?

KEV. Yeah.

BREN *exits. The door shuts behind him.*

EDDIE. You – You could've made a bit of an effort Kevin. Look at the cut of you.

KEV. Oh right.

EDDIE. For your mother's sake – you're scruffy-looking.

KEV. Right.

EDDIE. . . . Well, will you clean up or something?

KEV. Yeah – okay.

KEV *gets up.*

EDDIE. Not now. Sit down – will you?

KEV. Oh right.

KEV *sits down.*

EDDIE. Why aren't you paying me back Kevin? I'm waiting on you.

KEV. . . . Yeah – I'm just – kind of – finding my feet.

EDDIE. Sure you're there six months now.

KEV. It might be five – I think.

EDDIE. I'd like that money back now Kevin – you know? You can pay me off in instalments – I'd prefer the lump but if that's all you can do then, I don't mind – all right?

KEV. . . . Yeah – yeah – I will – I'll do that then – that's what I'll do – thanks.

EDDIE. So when can I expect my first cheque?

KEV. Your first cheque? That would be – I'd say, probably in about two weeks, two weeks I'd say.

EDDIE. Two weeks – right – I'll be standing at the letter box with my hand out.

KEV. Right.

EDDIE. . . . You're getting on fine there now anyway – are you?

KEV. Yeah.

EDDIE. That's good.

KEV. . . . Yeah . . . Well.

EDDIE. . . . What?

KEV. No it's nothing.

> ANDY *enters. The door shuts behind him. He has been in the bathroom trying to tidy himself up (e.g. wetting and combing his hair). He is self-conscious about the cut on his forehead and might be trying to hide it.*

ANDY. How're you Da?

EDDIE. What – What happened your head?

ANDY. What?

EDDIE. Your big bloody mouth again – was it?

ANDY. No, no – this morning – you know the – the 'filled-in' canal there. Remember you were thrown into it once but there was no water so you didn't drown or anything.

EDDIE. What?

ANDY. Yeah – this morning there at the canal – some young-fella up behind this young-one he was – he had her by the hair – lashing her head off the wall – he was – so – I had to jump in and next minute the two of them are lashing into me and then these junkies like out of nowhere with hurlies cleaned me out – you see the whole thing was a set-up – the lashing into her and all that.

EDDIE. . . . You – They cleaned you out?

ANDY. Yeah – you see life is cheap and the rich get richer and all that – it's what this country's coming to – everyone's talking about it. So how are you anyway, you're looking well.

EDDIE. Is this a joke you're telling me – is that it?

ANDY. What – what joke? – This happened.

> BREN *enters from the kitchen.*

But these were very professional fellas – not like in your day – that's what I'm saying.

BREN (*to* EDDIE). The kettle's boiled. There's a tea bag in the cup but there's no milk. Someone (*i.e.* ANDY) drank the milk. So if you want it black – it's in there but don't throw the tea bag in the sink – throw it in the bin – cos it'll stain it – it's only a new sink – I don't want it stained.

EDDIE. . . . What? (*To* ANDY.) You – don't be going mental – on me today – do you hear me?

ANDY. I'm not going mental. How d'you / think I got this (*indicates the cut*)?

EDDIE. Where's Deirdre?

ANDY. . . . Deirdre? She's – she's shopping – now.

EDDIE. Shopping? But – she is coming?

ANDY. Yeah . . . well she – she – she's not quite sure – like she's a lot of things on today – she said.

EDDIE. She's a lot of 'things on'? What? What does that mean?

ANDY. It's – but – like – why do you want her over anyway?

EDDIE. What? I said – with Gordon – your mother – she wants to see them.

ANDY. . . . Yeah – it's just – she's a lot on – today. (*To* EDDIE.) So how's / Ma?

EDDIE. I left a message on your phone!

ANDY. . . . What? Yeah – I know.

EDDIE. But – where is she?

ANDY. Yeah. She knows about it all right.

EDDIE. What? Of course she knows – what're you saying to me?

ANDY. That she knows we're here but that we might be better off just going over ourselves.

EDDIE. What? I asked for Deirdre and Gordon.

ANDY. I know.

EDDIE. Well what then – where is she?

ANDY. Well what she said to me was that she'll try and make it – so if she comes – she comes kind of thing.

EDDIE. She – what? When's that gonna be?

ANDY. Well four o'clock you said so – like when are the visiting hours in the hospital?

EDDIE. Did she say 'four o'clock' – is that what she said?

ANDY. Yeah – four o'clock she said – she knows it and she'll come.

EDDIE. What? Well what? Why didn't you say that?

ANDY. I thought I did say that.

EDDIE. No that's not what you said.

ANDY. Right. I didn't say that – I thought I did though.

EDDIE (*to* BREN). Would you have something to drink Brendan – anything?

BREN. What – 'drink' drink – do you mean?

EDDIE. What? Water! Anything! Kevin – get me a glass of water – would you? Thanks.

KEV. Right.

    KEV *exits into the kitchen.*

EDDIE. One small thing – I ask you to do – like – how hard can it be?

ANDY. Well it's just people are busy – it's not like the old days with housewives and all that.

EDDIE. What're you talking about?

ANDY. Nothing.

EDDIE. And she'll bring Gordon then – won't she?

ANDY. . . . Well he wouldn't be anywhere except with Deirdre – d'you know what I mean?

EDDIE. Yeah well could you ring her then to make sure?

ANDY. Yeah I did ring but she's out all day now so like – she'll be making her way over here then when the time comes – d'you know what I mean?

BREN. When did you ring?

ANDY. You were asleep.

EDDIE. I want us all to go over – let your mother know what's at home for her – all right?

ANDY. Right.

EDDIE. Right . . . so . . . how's the welding going for you?

ANDY. Grand yeah – nights – you know.

EDDIE (*to* ANDY). You could do with cleaning yourself up a bit Anthony.

ANDY. Who me?

EDDIE. Yeah – look at you.

   KEV *returns with the water and hands it to* EDDIE.

   Thanks.

ANDY. Yeah – well I asked Bren if I could take a shower but he wouldn't let me.

   EDDIE *drinks some water with a thirst.*

BREN. No you didn't – he (*indicates* KEV) asked me. And I didn't say I wouldn't let him. I hadn't put the water on. I take a shower before I go to work. I'm usually asleep in my bed by now so there's no point in having it on.

EDDIE (*to* BREN). Will you just get him a clean shirt?

BREN. Right.

EDDIE. Look I don't care what you wear – but your mother will look at you and think you're homeless. All right? And get him a pair of pants – as well.

ANDY. Pants?

EDDIE. They're manky – look at them.

ANDY. Right – pants – and then we'll go over – see how Ma is.

EDDIE. What? When Deirdre comes we'll go over.

ANDY. Well – you know – we could be waiting.

EDDIE. 'Four o'clock' you said?

ANDY. Yeah but time-keeping with Deirdre – like – she doesn't have a job anymore – she's forgotten how.

EDDIE. Well we'll wait till four.

BREN. Which hospital is it – Da?

EDDIE (*to* ANDY). What? Will you – will you get changed? (*To* BREN.) Then we can talk about hospitals – all right?

ANDY (*to* BREN). Where's your wardrobe?

BREN. I'll get them.

BREN *gets up.*

EDDIE (*to* BREN). And get him (*indicates* KEV) an outfit as well – will you?

KEV. Me? We're not all the same size Da – you know?

EDDIE. What's your problem?

KEV. It's – it's gonna look weird cos like Ma'll know / I'm wearing *his* (*indicates* BREN's) clothes.

EDDIE. All your mother sees is dirt Kevin. She won't even know what you're wearing – as long as it's clean. (*To* BREN.) Go on then.

BREN. . . . Right.

BREN *exits. The door shuts behind him.* KEV *is sulking.* ANDY *is conscious of the cut.* EDDIE *takes some more water.*

EDDIE. . . . Right . . . Okay. (*Pause.*) Right – look – the thing is – your mother – your mother . . . your mother – misses you – all right? You don't ring her enough. Kevin does – fair play . . . But she'd still like to see you – I mean – she's very proud of all your achievements and all that but she's your mother – you see – there's only me and her now and . . . so – every now and then – Kevin – you should be coming home, especially you Kevin – you were the last to leave, do you understand – give her your good news?

KEV. Yeah.

EDDIE. And Anthony – she just – with you – she just likes to see you – with Gordon and Deirdre – altogether like – the three of yis – and – you could ring her an odd time as well – you know?

ANDY. I do ring her but it's just like when she's talking antibiotics – I don't know what to be saying to her. 'Yeah take them Ma – that's good – keep taking them' – you know?

EDDIE. It's nothing to do with what she's saying Anthony – it's just talk – just say 'yeah' every now and then – can you do that?

ANDY. That's what I do do.

EDDIE. And she wants to see Gordon – you don't understand that – he's her first grandchild / Anthony.

ANDY. Yeah I know.

EDDIE. Bring him over then.

ANDY. Right.

BREN *enters. The door shuts behind him. He is dressed in his uniform and has clothes for* ANDY *and* KEV *which are similar in type and colour to his uniform.* BREN *puts down the neatly folded clothes.*

BREN. There you go.

ANDY. . . . These are your casual clothes?

BREN. Do you have a problem with that?

EDDIE. Just put them on.

ANDY. No – no – I'm not complaining. Right.

> ANDY *starts to undress.* KEV *picks up the clothes with reluctance.*

EDDIE. And you Brendan – you should call over an odd time as well – / you know – chat.

KEV (*to* BREN). Where's your jacks?

BREN. What? Through there.

> KEV *exits with the clothes.*

EDDIE. Like Sunday dinner once a month Brendan – you can do that – can't you?

BREN. Sunday dinner?

EDDIE. You've no time for your mother – is that it?

BREN. . . . I pick up the phone to her – don't I?

EDDIE. So, it's an ordeal for you – is that what you're saying?

BREN. No. It's not – no. Right.

EDDIE. Sunday dinner then.

BREN. Right.

EDDIE. Right. Grand – right – now – the other thing is – is – that – she'd like a photograph of us all together – a nice family photograph.

ANDY. A photograph? Did she say that?

EDDIE. Yeah she did.

ANDY. When?

EDDIE. What? Just there – recently she did.

ANDY. Why's that – I wonder?

EDDIE. What – cos – what? Cos everyone has them. When you have your grandchild you take the photograph – the generations and we'll get dressed up – all right?

ANDY. Did she say this after she was brought into hospital or was it before?

EDDIE. What? This is just something she was talking about.

ANDY. And she wants to get it done quickly enough – does she?

EDDIE. Well I think we could with the – sun still shining – get it done.

ANDY. Before the summer's over kind of thing?

EDDIE. So can we do that then – split four ways? You (*to* BREN) could organise it – couldn't you?

BREN. . . . If I got the money up front.

EDDIE. I don't think that'd be a problem – would it?

ANDY. You want us all to pay for it?

EDDIE. Well, you're all going to be in the thing!

ANDY *is dressed.* KEV *enters in* BREN*'s clothes. He is still sulking.*

ANDY. Hah! Give us a twirl there Kev.

EDDIE. They're grand.

BREN. So what's wrong with Ma?

EDDIE. What? She's – what? – She's lonely since Kevin left – and when her friend died, Mrs C. the invalid – she took that very badly and her chest is bad and she's going to that same doctor now – that chancer – it was that menopause did it to her – she was never right after it – you – you just don't know where you are with her but it's just something they all have to go through but now – you see she's doing this job, part-time, looking after retarded children or they're not retarded – they're what?

BREN. Disturbed.

EDDIE. Disturbed children from broken homes. She's doing that cos she says she needs to occupy herself but she's not able for it anymore – I mean didn't she bring yous up?

ANDY. But – so her chest is bad then – is it?

EDDIE. Yeah well she has had this cough now for a while – / you know yourself?

BREN. Is it James's hospital she's in?

ANDY. So is that what she's in with then – that floored her – did it – the chest?

EDDIE. . . . Well no – this is more of a – a menopause . . . thing.

BREN. Ma had a hysterectomy Da.

EDDIE. Yeah what? Of course she had.

BREN. The menopause is a different thing.

EDDIE. What? How long have you been married Brendan?

BREN. Sorry?

EDDIE. Don't be getting smart with me.

BREN. I'm not getting smart.

EDDIE. . . . Look there's side effects to these operations and – that's why – well – the other thing is – is that – what your mother needs is a holiday. We haven't gone away now for a few years and you know your mother always wanted . . . a – a mobile home on the Strand. So I can't afford it but there's no reason why we can't all just chip in and buy one for her. Take her away for a few months. A second-hand one is all I'm talking about – which – cos I rang up a fella – it'd only be about two grand or so each and you're all earning good money now so it shouldn't be a problem to you. (*Pause. Nobody responds.*) What? (*Pause.*) So that's all right then – is it? Grand.

BREN. . . . That's a lot of money Da.

EDDIE. You just got promoted – so I'll have none of that.

BREN. I've a mortgage / to pay.

EDDIE. This is for your mother – Brendan you wouldn't do that for her?

ANDY. So – is this like – you just want us to agree this – before we go over – is that it?

EDDIE. So we'll have a nice surprise for her.

ANDY. So we go over and we tell her about this and then she'll tell us the story cos you can't – cos she told you not to – but we won't say anything if you tell us – we won't.

BREN. What?

ANDY. I know you don't want to talk about it Da but like – can you say – like – there is money there – isn't there?

EDDIE. Are you concussed or something?

ANDY. What? No – but – right – okay – fair enough – well why don't we just go over there now then – instead – cos then we could spend more time with Ma herself – do you know what I mean?

EDDIE. . . . We're waiting on Deirdre and Gordon.

ANDY. I know. But sure Deirdre and Gordon can go see her another day.

EDDIE. I want yis all over today – I told you.

ANDY. I know – but four o'clock if she's not here – then we'll have to go – you know – time-wise.

EDDIE. But she will be here – you said she would.

ANDY. Yeah. I know.

EDDIE. Right. So – we'll wait.

ANDY. Right.

EDDIE. Right. So that's settled then – is it? I'll start looking out for one – two grand each – right.

ANDY. Yeah – sure we could even take the photograph outside the mobile home. Like a kind of a new home for us now that we're all grown up and everything? That'd be good – wouldn't it? . . .

EDDIE. A nice, clean white one – hardly used – is what I'm thinking of.

BREN (*to* KEV). You're all right with that Kev – are you? Two grand?

KEV. Well see the thing is – what I was gonna say to you Da was that cos it's an American company I work for – the thing is that there's word going round that they're gonna actually have to lay off some people – that's the thing.

EDDIE. But sure you're only just in there.

KEV. I know but it's an international thing – it probably won't affect us but they're saying it might all the same.

EDDIE. So what're you saying exactly?

KEV. I'm saying that the job – that the job I have – that it's not one hundred per cent secure as a job – the one I'm in – it's not so secure as that.

EDDIE. No job's one hundred per cent secure – where did you hear that?

KEV. Yeah.

EDDIE. For God's sake – Kevin – grow up – will you?

KEV. . . . Right.

EDDIE. Look I want to come out of here today knowing that this is all sorted – so can I get an agreement on that then?

BREN. We need to know which hospital it is – Da?

EDDIE. Will you / will you just?

ANDY. Yeah Bren'll be court-martialled if he's late – won't you?

BREN. If it's James's – I'd never make it back.

ANDY. And Gordon's going to be taking his nap by then Da – he'd be asleep.

EDDIE. Seeing him's enough.

BREN. Is it James's or the Mater or Beaumont – which is it?

EDDIE. I want this business sorted Brendan.

BREN. But which hospital is it?

EDDIE. Can I get this sorted?

BREN. Which hospital is it?

EDDIE. Will you just / will you?

BREN. Which hospital?

EDDIE. She's not – she's not in hospital – all right?

BREN. . . . She's not in hospital?

EDDIE. . . . Look – all right – I'll level with you. (*Pause.*)
I got home Monday morning and there was a note on the
kitchen table from your mother. And the note said that she
was staying at a friend's house, for a few days but not
to worry and that she'd ring – all right?

BREN. What? She'd ring – / what d'you mean?

EDDIE. Will you let me finish? So she rang then or that oul
one – her friend – Jess is her name – rang me on
Wednesday morning.

BREN. What does that mean – she's 'staying / at a friend's
house' – what does that mean?

EDDIE. This oul one said that your mother was with her – not
to worry and that she'd like to see me Friday afternoon –
she'd like to see us all Friday afternoon – all right?

BREN. She'd like to see us all or just you?

EDDIE. She'd like to see us all you see – she's taking a little
break – she's been down in the dumps since Mrs C. died.

BREN. So Ma's not in hospital – she's in this woman Jess's
house – she wants the whole lot of us over there – this
woman who we've never met and she's coming back the
weekend – tomorrow or Sunday – is that it? Cos that
doesn't make any sense.

EDDIE. I just want you to chip in on a mobile home – and to
agree that and then I want us all to go over to see your
mother. Is that too hard to understand?

BREN. Yeah well it is a bit.

ANDY. She's not in hospital?

EDDIE. She's down in the dumps.

BREN. Did she say she was 'down in the dumps'?

EDDIE. Jesus Brendan you've no clue – have you? (*To* ANDY.)
I mean does Deirdre say that to you Anthony? They don't –
they don't tell you these things – they just – and the next
minute she's throwing – cans of beans at you. And then –
you know – everything's dirty, everything's filthy dirty,
being alive is dirty to your mother! And then – then she just
lashes out. Sure – sure – she clattered you plenty of times.

ANDY. But she's not sick?

EDDIE. Sure didn't you lose your hearing once?

ANDY. Yeah for three days – I can still feel her hand on my
face – / but Da.

EDDIE. She doesn't mean any harm by it – / that's just what
she does.

ANDY. But she wasn't a very loving mother – I mean when
you hear about these mothers – you know like – she never
made Rice Krispie buns – do you know what I mean?
'TLC' and all that – what they talk about – the mothers –
the good mothers and the fathers.

EDDIE. What's your problem?

ANDY. I'm just saying that when you see the Da like throwing
the stick to the dog and everyone's hugging each other and
all that – it makes you think – I mean we went to the
Paddy's Day parade once – like that was the only time we
ever went out together as a family like – wasn't it?

EDDIE. What – Paddy's Day? That – what? Yeah and – and –
what happened – you what? You rob some little kid's – what
do you call it? – rosette – and the next minute the guards
are down on us and – and – and – and why? Because of
some little scut – because of you – is it no wonder you
never got taken out?

ANDY. What – that – that – that's – that's because we never
were taken out – it was the whole – the shock of it – we just
didn't know what to be doing with ourselves.

EDDIE. Did you ever go a Christmas without a present?

ANDY. No – but like who does?

EDDIE. Did I ever raise my hand to you – did I?

ANDY. I'm not complaining Da – I'm just saying that . . .

EDDIE. What the hell are you on about?

ANDY. I don't know – just stuff – all right – is Ma sick or
what?

EDDIE. Look – right – we're not a perfect – no one is and
your mother – she just loses it every now and then.

ANDY. Yeah well Deirdre's the same Da – like there's no
logic.

EDDIE. No there's no logic and you don't know the half of it
lads – believe me – the abuse I've had to put up with. But
anyway – look – this – this Jess oul one's a bad influence on
her. She's a separated woman and she got her this job – a
job she doesn't need. So like – can we just go over there
and do that – remind her of what she's got at home.

ANDY. She's not a lezzer – is she? This Jess one?

EDDIE. What?

ANDY. Well you know these oul ones going round the place –
these dykes – is that what you mean – she's 'separated'?

BREN. Have you met her Da?

EDDIE. What? No – / I haven't met her.

BREN. She was at the funeral – you (*to* KEV) said?

KEV. Yeah.

BREN (*to* EDDIE). And you didn't go to the funeral, sure you
didn't?

EDDIE. I couldn't get off – bloody work – you – but you –
you met her Kevin.

KEV. Yeah.

EDDIE. Well – what's – what's she like?

KEV. She's tall.

EDDIE. Right – anything else about her besides her tallness?

KEV. Well she's not disabled or anything – sure she isn't?

EDDIE. Not that I know of no – so – what – anything else about her?

KEV. I didn't really notice her that much – she's old like – you know?

EDDIE. Older than your mother you mean?

KEV. No about the same age.

EDDIE. As me – like – about the same age as me?

KEV. Yeah – but – but you – you look young though.

BREN (*to* EDDIE). What do you mean – 'remind her of what she's got at home'?

EDDIE. Sorry?

BREN. That's what you said – we all go over and remind her of what's she's got at home.

EDDIE. Yeah, her home – her children – her grandchild.

BREN. Are you not getting on with each other at the moment Da – is that it?

EDDIE. What? She's going away for a few days – she asked to see you – that's all. End of story. Where's your jacks?

BREN (*to* EDDIE). So we go over there – we tell her how well we're doing and then you bring up the mobile home and she says 'great, okay I better leave here now, then' – is that it?

EDDIE. You're some smart-arse aren't you?

BREN. That's what you said.

EDDIE. I did not – where's your jacks?

BREN. In through there into the left.

EDDIE. Right.

> EDDIE *gets up.*

ANDY. So – there's no sickness at all – not even a slight one?

EDDIE. We just need to cheer her up Anthony – all right?

ANDY. No but – is it that it's too late for her to be going into hospital – that she'd rather be at home kind of thing except not our home – is that why there's no hospital?

EDDIE. No – / there's no hospital.

ANDY. But her chest?

EDDIE. Yeah well she is a bit wheezy all right.

ANDY. It's okay Da – you can tell us – me and Kev we're prepared for it.

EDDIE. Prepared for what?

ANDY. It's all right Da – we won't say anything to her – honest.

EDDIE. 'Say' – Say what?

ANDY. She – does she have cancer Da – Ma has cancer.

EDDIE. Cancer? What? Where did you get that idea?

ANDY. Because – cancer – because the suddenness – us all getting together – and but you know – it's all right because then – every cloud has a silver lining and the way – that cos she's settling her affairs.

EDDIE. Settling what affairs?

ANDY. After Mrs C.'s funeral and now cos of her cancer.

EDDIE. There is no cancer!

ANDY. But . . . well – how do you know?

EDDIE. I think she'd tell me if she had cancer Anthony.

ANDY. But no you're just saying that cos you want her to tell us herself – is that it?

EDDIE. How many times do I have to tell you – there's no cancer – 'n' – 'o' – 'no', no cancer.

ANDY. . . . . Right.

EDDIE *exits for the bathroom. The door shuts behind him.*

BREN. Where did you get that idea?

ANDY. Fuck.

BREN. What's wrong with you?

ANDY. She's sick – she was sick – she was – she was sick.

BREN. She had a chest infection.

ANDY. I thought she was dying.

KEV (*to* ANDY). But that's better – isn't it? She's just kind of depressed – like.

ANDY. What do you know?

BREN. Leave him alone.

ANDY. She's supposed to be dying.

KEV. But she won't be able to hear anything that might be depressing – if she's depressed will she?

BREN. Ma told me stuff.

ANDY. What? What stuff?

BREN. Personal stuff. I think I know what it is – it doesn't matter – I'm not going over anyway.

EDDIE *enters. The door shuts behind him.*

ANDY. What stuff?

EDDIE. No word from Deirdre yet – no?

BREN. This new job Ma's in Da – she gets paid for that – doesn't she?

EDDIE. What? A pittance – why?

BREN. But is it enough to live on like – by herself?

EDDIE. What're you talking about?

BREN. What's she earning?

EDDIE. Earning? Sure I pay her.

BREN. Yeah I know but this job it's not just pocket money for her – is it?

EDDIE. She doesn't need this job Brendan.

BREN (*to* EDDIE). I think you should just go over there yourself Da.

EDDIE. What?

BREN. You don't want to go over alone so you've asked us along.

EDDIE. What? I don't want to go near yis Brendan – she asked for you – I even said it to her – I said 'would it not be better for me just to go over cos that's a lot of organising to do to get the lads together?' But she said 'no I want to see them all, I've a bit of news for them.'

ANDY. You didn't say she had news?

EDDIE. Well what else would she be bringing yis over for?

ANDY. What sort of news did she say?

EDDIE. She didn't say.

ANDY. Good or bad or what?

EDDIE. Oh I'd say it's good – the way she was talking about it.

ANDY. Yes! Yes! Yes! Yes! Yes!

EDDIE. What the hell?

ANDY. None of yis would fucking believe me – I told you!

EDDIE. What're you talking about?

ANDY. The money – Da – Mrs C. – good news – she's a widow – there was no-one at the funeral.

EDDIE. What?

ANDY. The will – Mrs C. – her house – she had no-one else – Ma was the only – at the funeral – Da – the money.

EDDIE. What?

ANDY. You don't have to tell me – it's all right – I won't say anything. How much did she get? I've been thinking about it for months.

EDDIE. Yeah, well.

ANDY. It's all right you don't have to tell me but like Mrs C. –
she was loaded and where did it all go? Of course it did –
who else? Jesus Da – it's fucking great!

BREN. What're you talking about?

ANDY. The 'good news' – Ma's money – Mrs C. – the funeral –
Bren – it's money.

BREN. What money?

ANDY. The funeral – why do you think we're all going over?

BREN (*to* EDDIE). Is this true?

ANDY. Of course it's true – ah Jesus Da – it's fucking brilliant –
thank you – Jesus – thank you.

EDDIE. . . . All right – look your mother – I – she doesn't
want me to say – just to tell you that it's good news and for
you all to come over.

ANDY. There's just so much that me and Deirdre / we want to –
to –

EDDIE. All right – okay.

ANDY. To spend it on. No Da it's great news.

EDDIE. All right – just keep it under your hat.

ANDY. It's great – I mean Kev – like – I mean are you not
happy – Kev – like you know it's money?

KEV. Yeah but / I – I –

ANDY. Mrs C. – like it just goes to show – some people
appreciate having their nappy changed – do you know what
I mean? Twenty five years.

BREN (*to* EDDIE). But – so – Mrs C. gave everything over to
Ma? Her house and all her savings?

EDDIE. Now, well, look Brendan – I'm not supposed to be
saying anything except that it's good news / all right.

ANDY. And there's no cancer like – Ma's not dying which is
even better?

EDDIE. What? No – no there's no dying.

ANDY. You see cos I thought that like she was dying and that this was like because of that she was getting us altogether with the will before you know she loses it but that's even better now because she's – she's still okay – yes – yes – yes – yes – yes!

EDDIE. Okay – calm down Anthony.

ANDY. I mean so – does that mean that she's going to divide up the will when we go over now – or what?

EDDIE. What? I'm not supposed to say any more – I'm under instructions – all right?

ANDY. Yeah – yeah – no bother.

BREN. So this is what Ma's going to be telling us?

EDDIE. That's it. So just let me do the talking – you're not supposed to know anything.

KEV. Da?

EDDIE. What?

ANDY. See she was clever Ma – she stuck in there all those years cos she knew she was on a winner.

BREN. So why is Ma leaving it till now to tell us?

EDDIE. Because it's not something you want to go broadcasting – is it?

BREN. You don't know Ma if you think she can keep a secret.

EDDIE. Can you not accept a bit of good news for once Brendan?

ANDY. There was legal stuff to be gone through with solicitors and all that – I'd say – was there?

KEV. But like so there is money then – Mrs C. did give Mam her money then – is that it?

EDDIE. She did but I'm not supposed to say anymore – so all right – you know now and that's it.

KEV. Right – cos / you see like.

ANDY. Just the gaf alone would be worth a fortune – Da.

BREN. But why's Ma going over to this woman's house to tell us?

EDDIE. That's – she's just helping that woman out.

BREN. What d'you mean – helping her out?

EDDIE. It's a private thing – a woman's thing – it's something she has – an infection or something.

BREN. An infection?

ANDY. Look Bren if you don't want your share then I'm sure myself and Kev would look after it for you – wouldn't we? Kev?

KEV. Yeah but – I – / I just – you see –

EDDIE. Don't worry about it Brendan – we just have to go over and say nothing – can you do that?

ANDY. No problem – Da.

BREN. There's money waiting on us – a share of a will?

EDDIE. There is – yeah – so – grand – Deirdre and Gordon – will you ring her?

BREN. But why do we have to get a mobile home for her?

KEV. I – Da?

EDDIE. What?

BREN. Da?

EDDIE. I'm not answering any more questions on it – except that it's good news so just keep hush about it – all right. Phone Deirdre.

BREN. And we're all getting an equal share of this money – you included Da – is that it?

ANDY. Well yeah – Ma – I'd say like cos me and Deirdre don't have a house yet – you (*to* BREN) do kind of thing

and you've no kids – I'm sure Ma'll have it worked out –
who gets what and all that. Like we need a house and a car.

BREN. You made your bed Andy.

ANDY. What? What've you got to spend it on?

BREN. I have plans.

ANDY. Let's just go over now Da – come on – we'll just go.

EDDIE. What? But – we're waiting on Deirdre and Gordon?

ANDY. I know but she hasn't rung yet so I'd say that she's just
gonna be late so you know – I mean – I'll ring her tonight –
she'll be very happy with the news.

EDDIE. But I want Deirdre and Gordon.

ANDY. I know you do but it's all fine now.

EDDIE. Phone her – will you?

ANDY. Does she really have to be there?

EDDIE. But – what? I – I told you!

ANDY. I know you did but – all right look – okay . . .

EDDIE. What?

ANDY. I'll level with you Da – I – I got home the other day
and the thing about it is – is that Deirdre's in Limerick –
it's just a temporary thing – / you see.

EDDIE. You – she's – you – she's in Limerick?

ANDY. With her brother. It's just yeah – you see – / what
happened was –

EDDIE. Jesus Christ Anthony!

ANDY. It's just a money thing.

EDDIE. I don't believe this!

ANDY. We just – / had a bit of a row.

EDDIE. You told me Deirdre and Gordon were coming – we're
fucking sitting here!

ANDY. I know – / I know.

EDDIE. I left messages!

ANDY. No but see – / but with Ma's money.

EDDIE. I don't fucking believe you!

ANDY. No look – it's all right.

EDDIE. It's not 'all right' I asked for them to come over – you said they were coming over?

ANDY. I know but they weren't coming over – that's the thing.

EDDIE. But you said they were!

ANDY. I know but they weren't!

EDDIE. Jesus Christ are you thick?

ANDY. It's all right now we have the money!

EDDIE. What fucking money?

ANDY. Ma's money – / it just – it'll sort everything.

EDDIE. I want Deirdre and Gordon.

ANDY. I know but – that's just – Ma'll understand – Da.

EDDIE. You don't understand – they were supposed to be here – I fucking asked you for them!

ANDY. I know!

EDDIE. Jesus Christ.

ANDY. But Da we just had a bit of a row over money but now we have money so it's all – all right.

EDDIE. Oh Christ! Anthony – Jesus Christ.

ANDY. But it's – why's it so bad like I mean Mrs C. gave Ma her money – she can meet Deirdre another time?

EDDIE. You don't understand.

ANDY. What? . . . What?

EDDIE. She asked me for Deirdre and Gordon.

ANDY. I know but she can always see them.

EDDIE. She can't always see them.

ANDY. Why not?

EDDIE. Because they're in fucking Limerick!

ANDY. I'll tell Deirdre about the money.

KEV. Andy! Da!

ANDY *and* EDDIE. What?!

KEV. I – I –

EDDIE. What?!

KEV. That – at – that at Mrs C's funeral they were talking about money.

EDDIE. What? What about it?

KEV. No it was just because whether – that – it's – since . . .

ANDY. What are you talking about Kev?

KEV. Yeah it was just Mam and Jess – I don't know I might be wrong cos I just overheard it.

BREN. Overheard what?

KEV. That – cos – Mam was kind of upset in the pub and Jess was there comforting her and I heard her saying to Mam like – they were talking about 'Mrs C.' that – like that she was 'an oul wagon' and that Jess'd get her a job and 'not to worry' and Mam – Mam was saying 'don't speak ill of the dead' but Jess was saying 'she was an oul mean bitch not to give you anything' – something like that – but that – you see – that she gave all the money to an animal charity – for – I think it was donkeys. It was just cos – but whether it was different since because you (*indicates* EDDIE) said that there was money now? That's what I mean. You know different.

ANDY. Donkeys?

EDDIE. That's – yeah – no – there is money now / that was just at the time of the funeral.

ANDY. So what – so – what – that – that's not true then – what he said?

EDDIE. Well what's it to you – where's Deirdre?

BREN. It's true – Da – isn't it? There is no money?

ANDY. Did she get any money Da – yes or no?

EDDIE. You're a fucking disgrace.

ANDY. I need that money Da.

EDDIE. The only reason you're going over to see your mother is because there's money – is that it?

ANDY. No but you don't understand – / I need that money.

EDDIE. Well there is no fucking money – there's no money – all right!

ANDY. What?

BREN. Ah yeah.

EDDIE (*to* ANDY). So now – how do you feel about that? Twenty-five years fucking wiping that woman's arse and not so much as a 'thank you' – nothing. I told her not to be calling over to her – she's just using you I said – but your mother was having none of it.

BREN. So there's no money – that was a lie?

ANDY. But Da – the good news – like maybe she just hasn't told you yet – kind of thing?

EDDIE. Why would she not tell me?

ANDY. Well she might just – if – you know – that – she has the money now kind of thing – / so she can do what she likes – like.

BREN. You lied to us Da.

EDDIE. What the hell are you talking about – there's no fucking money!

ANDY. That she might be keeping it from you!

BREN. Kev overheard them Andy.

EDDIE. What? What's your problem Anthony?

ANDY. Cos Da – you don't know how much / I needed that money.

EDDIE. How much – what? Cop on – will you – there's no money! Fuck her. It doesn't matter – we'll survive. Come on we'll go on over.

ANDY. No – no Da – for Gordon – for to buy – for to buy a place.

EDDIE. But there never was any money.

ANDY. No but like – I was sure – it was definite – it was there – you rang.

EDDIE. So it's not there – save up for a place – Jesus Christ – that's what we all have to do – you have your job.

ANDY. Yeah but . . .

EDDIE. But what? Cop on – will you?

ANDY. I don't have a job anymore.

EDDIE. What d'you mean?

ANDY. I walked out last night – told the boss to screw it – screw her poxy job – 'fuck you' I said – you see – I thought there was money.

EDDIE. You what?

ANDY. I was giving it to Gordon – for a house – a big house with a swing – that's what I wanted so as he could have that.

EDDIE. But – but – but there – there never was any money?

ANDY. See I did this (*indicates his head*) to myself Da – I wasn't in a fight – I did this to myself.

EDDIE. What the hell?

BREN. Ah yeah.

ANDY. Deirdre's gone Da – she's gone to her brother's with Gordon – cos they have everything down there.

EDDIE. What? What're you talking about?

ANDY. Deirdre's depressed – it wasn't – she – there was
money owing – I've been working every night but you see
we lost the flat – cos – you see I – I mean. I mean now that
she's down there ⌐ like how am I going to see him? I said
all that – but she doesn't understand – she's in bed the
whole day she'd no idea – the same shit every night – for
what? But cos it was all fucked – in her pyjamas watching
telly – the whole thing – it just – we weren't even – having
you know – you see they have fields down there – they have
money and then you know that – I'm his father – that
doesn't fucking matter – no but look at where you come
from – she said.

As ANDY *speaks he starts banging his head off the wall
(*starting gently building to one or two big 'bangs'*) opening
up the wound that's there already.*

EDDIE. Ah Jesus Christ – stop – will you?

ANDY. No – Da – Jesus – I – you know – I want him there
and I'm telling him the answers – in the park with the dog –
we throw the stick to the dog – I do –

BREN. Here – watch me fucking wall!

ANDY. Jesus Christ he takes after me – and – I fucking love
him – but then – then – that's not gonna happen now – is
it? – cos – fucking money – cos – Jesus Christ – no see he's
better off now – cos he's with people now – they have the
money coming in – you see but – I love him Da – Jesus.

Blood is running down ANDY*'S face as he turns to the rest
of them.*

EDDIE. Ah – Christ Almighty – Jesus Christ!

BREN. Here – you're bleeding on my carpet.

EDDIE. Get him a towel.

BREN. Fuck's sake!

BREN exits into the kitchen. The door shuts behind him.

ANDY. I love him.

EDDIE. Ah Jesus Christ would you look at the state of you for crying out loud Anthony. There's more than just the two of you involved here – can you not work something out – get him back? Something normal – for fuck's sake – this'd break your mother's heart!

BREN *enters with a towel. The door shuts behind him.* ANDY *takes it from him.*

BREN. Here.

ANDY. But we're not normal.

EDDIE. You're his fucking father for Christ's sake!

ANDY. It's different these days – Deirdre's depressed / Da – you know?

EDDIE. Oh Jesus Christ – we're all fucking depressed – grow up – will you? Give her tablets – ask your mother – she takes them – / she's depressed.

ANDY. Deirdre doesn't want tablets.

EDDIE. You have to work at relationships Anthony – you know – you don't just give up – for Christ's sake! I mean – how long do you think – your mother and I are married?

ANDY. Well – what?

EDDIE. Yes we've had our rows but we're still together and that's because – because – most of all she's my best friend and I'm hers and yes – fair enough – she's depressed but underneath it all she's very happy. And that means something. None of yis will ever understand that – what it's like – none of yis are even right in the head to ever be in a relationship – Jesus Christ!

ANDY. It was all right for you – you could just come in and play your records.

EDDIE. What the hell are you talking about? Thirty years in the same job – did I ever complain? I have no pension. What am I going to live on when I retire? Have any of you ever once offered me money? Ever? I have to go and squeeze it out of you. Where's my money? . . . All right –

come on – fuck's sake – get yourself cleaned up – we'll say nothing to her – everything's fine – the mobile home – the photograph – all right? (*To* ANDY.) Get yourself cleaned up – tell her you walked into a lamp-post or something – right so – are we right Brendan?

BREN. I'm not going over Da.

EDDIE. . . . What? You are going over – we're all going over – so come on – lock up – let's go.

BREN. I think you should just go over there and sort it out between yis.

EDDIE. Sort what out? She asked to see yis – I told you.

BREN. You want us to crowd around you – cos she won't say anything to you when we're there.

EDDIE. What? What the hell?

BREN. Ma talks to me on the phone Da – you know – she tells me things.

EDDIE. What? What're you talking about?

BREN. I don't think you want to know.

EDDIE. What did she say to you?

BREN. She's told me personal things about you and I'd say now between one thing and another that she's had enough of you – that's what this is all about so, you know, it's between you two – not me – okay?

EDDIE. What 'personal' things?

BREN. I don't think you want to know Da – you know – really.

EDDIE. . . . Personal – personal what?

BREN. . . . She – right – well – she said that when you drink you wet the bed.

EDDIE. . . . You ungrateful little fucking bastard.

BREN. You piss in the bed when you drink.

EDDIE. After all I've done for you – Brendan.

BREN. You asked me.

EDDIE. You're some little fucking shite!

BREN. This is my house! I didn't ask you here and your fucking – family – fucking disputes – Jesus Christ.

EDDIE. Jesus what? It's not me it's your mother – she's – she's unstable in the head – / she's gone gaga.

ANDY. After all the grief you gave us as kids and now you're doing it?

EDDIE. I'm not – you fucking – you – yeah – everyone of you – you never stopped – a fucking specialist I got for him (*indicates* KEV). Jesus Christ the money you've cost me – fucking mattresses – the whole fucking lot of you.

ANDY. Get yourself put down after something like that Da – put down. That's disgraceful – it's embarrassing – Jesus.

EDDIE. Once it happened – once – and – and – and – it's never happened to you – bladders – no? – you – you – your fucking –

BREN. Ma's left you cos it happened once?

EDDIE. What's this 'left me' business – no-one's left me?

BREN. She's just taking a holiday up the road there – is that it?

EDDIE. What's your fucking problem?

ANDY. You piss in the bed Da – it's over – / you might as well do away with yourself.

EDDIE. You walk out of work – you leave your child / with no income whatsoever.

BREN. Could you please fucking leave?!

EDDIE. Look it – look it – we have to do something to get your mother away from that woman.

BREN. Please – could you just go now?

EDDIE. Yeah – come on – let's do that – let's go.

ANDY. Ma's had enough Da – that's it.

EDDIE. Come on – we'll go on over – come on.

BREN. I'm asking you nicely Da.

EDDIE. Your mother thinks you're a saint Brendan.

BREN. I don't care.

EDDIE. Well I'll tell her Brendan – will I?

BREN. Tell her what?

EDDIE. I'll tell her all about your dirty, filthy habits.

BREN. Tell her what you want – I don't care.

EDDIE. . . . Wanking over a pair of knickers – some little girl's knickers.

BREN. That's complete crap.

ANDY. Lorraine's knickers – were they?

EDDIE. I had to prize them out of his hands.

ANDY. That girl lost her marbles because of that and he was bullied over it – weren't you?

KEV. Just a little bit – but I forgive you.

ANDY. You should apologise to him Bren.

EDDIE. It's about time your mother was let in on some hard facts – Brendan.

BREN. Ma's left you Da – you know – she just doesn't feel like lying in it anymore – / I mean I don't blame her – she always had a thing about it.

EDDIE. I'll tell her Brendan – I will. I'll tell her.

BREN. Tell her what you like – she'll hate you all the more for it.

EDDIE. Well I will tell her – I'd be glad to tell her.

ANDY. Tell her she's a pervert for a son.

BREN. You fucking watch it!

EDDIE (*to* BREN). You're sick in the head – you need help.

ANDY (*to* EDDIE). What d'you think his computer's for?

EDDIE. What the – What're you watching on it (*indicates the computer*)?

BREN. This is my house – I don't have to take this crap in my house.

EDDIE. Just tell me that you're not watching anything illegal?

ANDY. Just adult women Bren – is it?

BREN (*to* ANDY). I take very serious offence to any allegations like that and if you keep it up I'll fucking plant you.

ANDY. Is it just tits and gees Bren?

BREN. I'm warning you Andy?

EDDIE. It's not kids Brendan – is it?

BREN. Fuck off out of my house!

EDDIE. Jesus Christ Brendan – you're a sick man – you should be locked up.

BREN. And what do you be doing in the boxroom Da?

EDDIE. I'll get the guards on you.

BREN. I seen you Da sure – sure – d'you / not remember?

EDDIE. They will – they'll take you away – they will.

BREN. 'Putting on records', turning up the volume – I know what you're at – I saw you.

EDDIE. You need help Brendan.

BREN. With your trousers down.

ANDY (*to* EDDIE). What?

BREN. I saw you – I was only a kid – you looked at me – d'you not remember?

ANDY. He was wanking?

BREN. I opened the door on you – I caught you.

EDDIE. Your mother is very proud of you Brendan.

BREN. You just looked at me and kept going.

ANDY. Jesus Christ Da! What the hell?

EDDIE. Don't mind him – fucking child fucking pervert –
molester.

BREN. I saw you – you just looked at me and you kept going.

EDDIE. I'm not a fucking pervert – fuck's sake – you walked
in – so what? It's only fucking human. Jesus Christ – a bit
of fucking privacy – in my own house. What do you think –
do you think I'd be – your mother – fuck's sake – you've no
clue – have you? Jesus Christ – she didn't want to have
anything to do with me – why do you think I? What? Fuck's
sake. No – fuck off – you're fucking – you haven't a
fucking clue – fuck off – if that's your attitude – you
fucking pervert – fuck off!

BREN. Get out of me house.

ANDY. You were pulling yourself off in the boxroom?

EDDIE (*to* ANDY). And you – you – you're fucking useless.
I'd be ashamed to have anything to do with you – the pair
of you!

ANDY. It's over Da – face up to it – Bren's right – Ma's left
you.

EDDIE. Fuck off – fuck's sake – fuck you – right – well right
so – the both of yis – right so – come on Kevin – your two
fucking perverted – fucking waster – fucking – fucking –
fuck off – fuck's sake – come on – they've let us down –
come on – so let's get over there – you and me – while we
still have our fucking pride left. (*Pause.* KEV *does not stir.*)
Come on – give her your good news. (*Pause.* KEV *does not
stir.*) What? (*Pause.* KEV *does not stir.*) What is it?

KEV. . . . Yeah

EDDIE. Yeah – yeah – yeah – what?

KEV. Yeah well see like – the thing is – I don't have – good
news.

EDDIE. What do you mean? Just tell her about Galway –
    that's enough – come on – we're late.

KEV. . . . Yeah but see – well – see – I – the thing is – what I
    was gonna tell Ma or tell you is that . . .

EDDIE. What?

KEV. I – I fell in love.

EDDIE. What? What? What're you talking about?

KEV. Yeah I mean that – what happened is that – I – I fell in
    love – I mean – I wanted to tell Mam to explain to her at the
    funeral – but cos well – see – on the phone like as well –
    you know – I haven't had a chance cos – it's hard and I
    thought then with this that – I could come back and tell her
    – but maybe now that – I don't think the time is right now
    for it if she's depressed – or maybe you could tell me where
    she is anyway?

EDDIE. I – I – I don't know what you're talking about Kevin.

KEV. I meant to tell Mam about it but cos I don't know now
    like if that's going to work so probably I should tell you
    really – I think.

EDDIE. What? Tell me what?

KEV. It's – it's – it's just a money thing as well, I mean I'll
    sort it out – it's just money a thing – it's just your money
    for the fees really – isn't it?

EDDIE. What is?

KEV. It's just – see I – I fell in love.

EDDIE. What's this falling in love – what the hell are you
    talking about?

KEV. Galway – it's about Galway.

EDDIE. What about Galway?

KEV. Yeah see – see . . .

EDDIE. . . . Oh Jesus Christ – don't tell me you were made
    redundant – is that it?

KEV. No – no – I wasn't – no.

EDDIE. Well what then? What? What?

KEV. Yeah see . . .

EDDIE. . . . What? You're a 'homo'?

KEV. No – no – I fell in love with this girl.

EDDIE. She's pregnant – is that it?

KEV. No – no she's not.

EDDIE. What then? What?

KEV. I – when I was here in college at a party I met this girl –
she lives in Galway. Noeleen is her name.

EDDIE. What? You have the clap – she's under-age – you're
getting married – what?

KEV. No – no.

ANDY. She's a transsexual? Noeleen is really Noel – no?

KEV. No – I fell in love with her. She's great – she makes her
own clothes and everything and she's into art and she was
just so nice and we stayed up the whole night – / the first
night.

EDDIE. Do I have to know this Kevin?

KEV. Yeah you do – you do.

BREN (to KEV). Could you not just tell him on the way cos I
have to get ready for work?

EDDIE. You met this girl – you fell in love – she broke your
heart – is that it?

KEV. I met her at this party and we kept in touch and you
know – I've never met anyone like her before she just – she
said – you don't *have* to do anything if you don't want to –
nobody's forcing you – you don't have to do it.

EDDIE. Do what?

KEV. See . . . I hated my course – I hated it. Every day going
in there – I hated it. I only ever went to college because of

you (*to* EDDIE) – because you always said that all work is crap but you just have to get on with it – that's why I did it. But I've stopped doing it. I'm not doing it anymore.

EDDIE. . . . You left college – I know you left college.

KEV. Yeah, but see I kept in touch with Noeleen and she said that I should come over if I was so – like – so depressed – that – because – life's too short and you have to live in the 'here and now' – and it's not easy but I'm trying – and – and you don't have to work at a shitty job or go to a shitty college and she said that there was plenty of room in her house – so that's what I did.

EDDIE. . . . What? You did what?

KEV. I'm sorry but you know – it was just – there was a lot of pressure and with you and with everyone expecting like – I don't know – for me to be like someone – that I'm not – kind of thing – and then the further it went on then – the worse it got – you know and I've been trying to tell Mam but – like she doesn't really want to hear like I mean – I had to tell you about the computer firm because you wouldn't have let me go – to – to Noeleen – obviously – I mean – otherwise – I mean – I'm sorry I had to do it but I had to – cos – and anyway it wouldn't ever have worked out with a computer firm so I'm sorry but that's – that's what happened – sorry.

EDDIE. . . . I'm not with you Kevin.

ANDY. You're not a big shot?

EDDIE. You don't work in computers? Is that what you're saying?

KEV. Yeah – no I mean – I don't.

EDDIE. Well – where do you work?

KEV. Yeah well see that's the thing – that – see Noeleen lives in a warehouse kind of a thing and see when I got there she already had a boyfriend. See – she didn't think – I don't think that she sort of knew about – how I felt for her – kind of thing.

EDDIE. . . . . What? Right. She has a boyfriend – so what?

KEV. Well it kind of meant something to me – I mean – it was a bit of a shock to me.

EDDIE. You didn't answer me Kevin – you're not in computers – so what are you in?

KEV. . . . Yeah – I'm – see her boyfriend like – when I ran out of money – he sort of lent me a drum kind of a thing and I sort of busk a bit with some other fellas – on the street – it's all right like it's not too bad but I think – well I do – I want to come back home now cos – well I don't really like being around her now and anyway she's going to be moving away soon so – it's like – you know – a like – a learning experience for me and I – what I want to do now is – I want to save some money and go to Australia and get a job over there – so that's the situation as it stands – right now. That's my plan and I was kind of hoping then that you could kind of break it to Mam for me but maybe not at the moment or today – kind of thing.

ANDY. Oh my God Kev – my God.

BREN. I knew there was something dodgy about you all right – all this American stuff – it just didn't add up.

EDDIE. . . . . I paid for your education Kevin – what were you doing – all that time?

KEV. I just followed my heart – she's beautiful like if you saw her – she has a bicycle and – but she has a boyfriend. I just made a mistake – that's all.

ANDY. Some fucking mistake / that – what?

EDDIE. Are you trying to kill me – is that it? Jesus Christ – do you know how many people your mother's told about you? You're the pride of the whole fucking neighbourhood.

KEV. She doesn't seem to be that interested whenever I talk to her.

EDDIE. What? She lives for you – Jesus Christ – the whole neighbourhood's driven demented with you.

KEV. Yeah.

BREN. All right. Is that it then – can you go now?

EDDIE. . . . And what about me? What about my hopes for you? Did you ever even think about that? About me? No – you didn't.

KEV. You wouldn't have listened to me if I told you.

EDDIE. So it's all my fault now – is it?

KEV. No – I'm just – I'm sorry – it was just – letting you down – I mean – I just – I did get very low like – I was nearly going to – you know – like – you know?

ANDY. Top yourself?

BREN. Ah Jesus.

EDDIE. Jesus Christ.

KEV. I just wanted to tell Mam – and you as well – and to ask you for your forgiveness and to start again then.

EDDIE. You want me to forgive you? What use is that?

KEV. Well it's just a sort of a healing thing.

EDDIE. Healing? And you expect me now to tell your mother all this and to ask her to forgive you – do you?

BREN. I have to get going Da.

KEV. Well I just thought you could like break it to her kind of thing – but not today obviously with the way things have happened.

EDDIE. How much is that going to cost me now – this – this forgiveness – how much?

KEV. I'm sorry.

EDDIE. You know when I look at you Kevin – that's all I see now – all the sacrifices – everything we could've had but don't . . . Could you not just have said something? That you didn't like your course?

KEV. No I couldn't – we never – sort of . . .

EDDIE. What?

KEV. Talked about these things.

EDDIE. Ah grow up – for fuck's sake you stupid – fucking
waster – Jesus Christ – you're bone fucking stupid.

KEV. I wanted / to tell you but –

EDDIE. What're you gonna do – you're gonna live off us now
for another few years – is it – I've to keep paying out for
you – is that it?

KEV. Well see I was kind of hoping like if I could come back
home but see maybe cos Mam isn't there – maybe you're
going to move out or something – I don't know.

EDDIE. What're you talking about – I'm not moving out.
When did I say that?

KEV. You didn't – I just sort of thought – the way it was going
that – that – that might happen.

EDDIE. You thought that – Jesus – are you retarded or
something – Christ Almighty? Stick to the redundancy story
when you're talking to your mother. That you're gonna be
made redundant, hint at it, fuck's sake – she thinks you're
brilliant. The only one of us that's ever had any brains –
I knew it was too good to be true – you're the worst of the
lot of them – Jesus Christ – some posh little fucking tart
flashes her tits at you and you go running after her – Christ
Almighty – have you no cop on – none of you? Go back
to Galway – stay over there until you sort something out –
I don't care. You'd give her heart failure. You're a drug
addict as well I suppose – are you?

KEV. No.

EDDIE. And I'm supposed to be grateful for that – am I? . . .
God Almighty . . . Right. Is that it then? Is there anything
else you want to tell me?

KEV. No.

EDDIE. Right we'll get going then – come on – we'll go over.

BREN. Yeah right – grand – you as well Anthony.

EDDIE. . . . What? Come on.

BREN. Come on lads – I've to go to work?

KEV (*mumbles*). . . . I'm not going over.

EDDIE. Speak up – will you? I can't hear you.

KEV. I'm not going over.

EDDIE. What?

KEV. I think you should go over on your own – I think it'd be better that way.

EDDIE. Do you now?

KEV. Yeah. I think that Da – that like all that stuff – it's not good Da – your bladder and everything.

EDDIE. Kevin you're too young you don't understand these things. Come on, just the two of us?

KEV. No I'm not going.

EDDIE. Right – so you're refusing me now as well Kevin – are you?

BREN (*pause*). Right Da – that's it then – none of us are going over – all right?

EDDIE. . . . No – no – look – look – all right . . . look –
I know I'm not the best father in the world – I know that but you know – I mean for your mother's sake. Come on I'm asking you . . . Please? . . . Look – your mother – your mother just wants more from life or something – I don't know – I mean – I'm happy enough having a few jars and you know – falling asleep – going to work and . . . I'm not doing that – that – you've the wrong idea . . . I – look we've worked out something together but your mother wants a bit more so – so that's why I just wanted to do this for her – a nice photograph of us and a place to go to on the Strand – cos you see – cos that's – that's where it all started really you see – we used to go for drives and – and – we were good looking – it was all very romantic . . . and then . . . then we got married – as people did in those days and then – then we had you Brendan and then we got the house and

then – we had you – Anthony and then – you – Kevin – you
know? But that's where it all started – the Strand – you see?
That's why – she likes it there – romance – you know –
so . . . I don't think I've been a bad father – I did my best –
we were young . . . we all change . . . I just want a quiet
life – you know? . . . Look . . . this – this – all this stuff
with my bladder – it's all – it happens – all the time – it
happens to men – I mean it happens to young-fellas – it's
not the age I am – it's just once or twice it let me down . . .
but I mean – this is a very private thing – so like – you
know I've stood by you all – you're my children and we're
very proud of you – so I mean – could you please return the
favour and stand by your old fella and go over with me –
that's all I'm asking you to do – this one thing? (*Long
Pause.*) That's it then – is it? That's a 'no' then – is it?
That's a 'no'? (*Long Pause.*) Right. (*Long Pause.*) She's left
me – is that it? (*Pause.*) Right. Right.

Pause. EDDIE *exits. The door shuts behind him.*

Lights down.

Scene Four

Lights up. Early evening. ANDY, KEV, BREN. ANDY *presses
the towel up to his head. Pause. All sitting in silence.*

ANDY. . . . What d'you reckon? . . . Is he fucked now or
what? . . . What do you think he's gonna say? Or is he
going over there at all – what d'you think? . . . You
wouldn't have a headache tablet Bren – would you?

BREN. No.

BREN *exits for the kitchen. The door shuts behind him.*

ANDY. . . . No more than he deserved anyway – is he out on
his ear – or what? . . . Kev?

KEV. I don't know.

ANDY. . . . You're a gas man – do you know that? Telling me
lies – you don't even have a girlfriend – you don't even
have a job – you're worse than I am . . . Jesus Kev . . . Well
you got rid of him – I suppose that's something . . . 'I fell in
love' – huh!

BREN *returns with a cloth and cleaner to wipe away any
traces of* ANDY's *blood on the wall. The door shuts behind
him. There may also be some blood on the floor which he
can try to clean away.*

(*Watching* BREN.) . . . Did I do any damage? I put a dent in
a door last night. You should've seen it.

BREN. Yeah – I've to go to work lads – so – you know if you
could get going?

ANDY. She'll kick him out of the gaf Bren – will she – what
do you reckon?

BREN. I don't know.

ANDY. If she could do that – I don't know – bar him – and sell
the gaf and move in with your woman? . . . Is Ma making
much at that job do you think? . . . Bren?

BREN. I don't know.

ANDY. Your woman Jess – she isn't dying or anything sure she
isn't? . . . Kev?

KEV. What?

ANDY. Did she look like she had any money? . . . Kev?

KEV. . . . She . . . no.

ANDY. She could do though . . . What do you think of Kev's
'falling in love' Bren – did he make your woman up or
what?

BREN. Will you get going cos I've to head off?

BREN *exits with cloth into the kitchen. The door shuts
behind him.*

ANDY. You made her up – didn't you?

KEV. Do you think that – I was thinking that – maybe – we could go over to see Mam – what d'you think?

ANDY. You just made her up?

KEV. No I didn't.

ANDY. So what? You got there and some bloke's on top of her with his kecks down and he's coming all over her and you did nothing? The 'love of your life'? You just let him away with it? Or were you into it? . . . Kev? . . . I'd've kicked him to Sunday.

KEV. . . . I set fire to a bin.

ANDY. . . . Did you? A bin? . . . What kind of a bin?

KEV. On the street – a public bin.

ANDY. A public bin?

KEV. I'd been thinking about it for ages and then I bought some fire-lighters.

ANDY. Like on the street?

KEV. Yeah – at night. I had a hat on.

ANDY. What did you do that for?

KEV. I'd been thinking about setting fire to a lot of things.

ANDY. Why didn't you just burn the drum he lent you?

KEV. Yeah – I don't know – I didn't want to upset Noeleen – I suppose.

ANDY. But sure she's after breaking your heart – man.

KEV. It's not really like that.

ANDY. A public bin – that's vandalism – Kev.

KEV. . . . Yeah but it was good.

BREN enters. The door shuts behind him.

BREN. All right lads – I've to go to work.

ANDY. Yeah, any chance of a few quid Bren? Cos I've got to go across town and get my wages?

BREN. . . . You think you'll still have wages?

ANDY. Yeah – why not? . . . Just the taxi fare and I'll be out the door.

BREN. I don't have it – sorry. So can you get going?

KEV. Bren? You know the way like Mam, like – why don't we just go over ourselves – visit Mam ourselves – see how she is?

BREN. . . . Not today – I've to go to work.

KEV. Yeah but – would you be into it – just the three of us – like?

BREN. I'll see her myself during the week – if she rings – if I get a chance – all right?

KEV (*to* ANDY). Yeah well, would you be interested in going over with me – later on – today like?

ANDY. Well I've to go in and get my wages.

KEV. What about tomorrow then?

ANDY. Yeah I might do – I can't promise you anything but.

KEV. Well maybe on Sunday because you won't be working on Sunday – will you?

BREN. . . . I have plans for Sunday – all right?

KEV. Yeah – see – you know the way like this is a two-bedroomed like I was sort of wondering if it would be possible to like – stay over here till – for – I mean – Sunday – then maybe we could go over – together.

BREN. One day would lead to two days – Kev – it wouldn't work. Go back to Galway and get a job. You heard what Da said – you know – really – you'd be better off keeping all this shit away from Ma – don't let her know what happened – just let it settle for a while.

ANDY (*to* KEV). That's telling you anyway – what?

KEV. Yeah but see I don't have a return ticket.

BREN. But sure how were you going to get back?

KEV. I – well I wasn't thinking of going back – I was going to go over to Mam and I thought that maybe I could stay here but . . .

BREN. You can't stay here Kev.

KEV. Do you know where this house is Ma's staying in?

BREN. No.

KEV. Do you?

ANDY. No.

KEV. Right.

BREN. . . . Well you can't stay here Kev – sorry – but no.

KEV. Right.

ANDY. Let him kip on the sofa for a night or two.

BREN. I wouldn't be doing you a favour Kev – really it wouldn't work out.

ANDY. Well at least give him his fare back to Galway.

BREN. . . . Right.

BREN *exits into the bedroom. The door shuts behind him.*

ANDY (*to* BREN *off*). Seeing as you're getting some you can get some for me as well – just a tenner – Bren'll do. I'll give it back to you. You can have your clothes.

KEV. Oh yeah.

ANDY *takes the towel from his forehead and with* KEV *they start taking off* BREN's *clothes and getting into their own.*

ANDY. So mean – isn't he?

KEV. Yeah.

ANDY. I'm glad to get out of these – I'll tell you that much.

KEV. Yeah.

ANDY. God knows what he does be doing in them.

KEV. Huh.

ANDY. . . . So you'll be going back to Noeleen then –
    anyway?

KEV. . . . No she's moving away.

ANDY. And you're not going to go with her – no? Tagging
    along like – no?

KEV. No.

ANDY. . . . I'd give you money Kev only I've just a few bob
    on me now for the few pints tonight – and I'm fucked then
    if I don't get paid – you know?

KEV. . . . Yeah.

ANDY. . . . Would you be into going for a pint with me like we
    could go to a night club.

KEV. . . . No it's all right – thanks.

ANDY. Are you sure?

KEV. Yeah – thanks.

ANDY. I'm going to get so pissed tonight – it's the only way –
    you know – I might even meet someone – what d'you
    reckon? Noeleen's little sister or something – does she have
    a sister? (KEV *does not respond*.) I'm only messing Kev.

    ANDY *and* KEV *finish undressing/dressing* – ANDY *puts
    the towel back up onto his forehead.*

    This (*indicates the cut on his head*) doesn't look too bad –
    does it?

KEV. . . . No I suppose not.

ANDY. Ah you know yourself the oul war wound always goes
    down well – I'll make up something – like I stopped a
    granny being mugged – or two grannies from a gang with
    knives and a dog – you know yourself?

KEV. Yeah.

ANDY. Jesus cheer up Kev – will you? Sure – you never know –
    you might get to Australia – someday – what?

    BREN *enters. The door shuts behind him.*

BREN. Right. Here.

> BREN *hands* KEV *money.*

ANDY. Anything for me – no?

BREN. No. Right – is that it – then?

> ANDY *hands out the towel for* BREN *to take.*

ANDY. Here.

BREN. I don't want it.

ANDY. You won't get any germs from it – it's just a bit of blood.

> BREN *takes the towel from* ANDY *holding it up by a corner.*

BREN. Right – okay – can you get going lads?

ANDY. So there's no room at the inn then for the pyromaniac – no?

BREN. Sorry?

ANDY. Set fire to a bin – he did.

BREN. Right – okay – is that it then?

ANDY. He's a vandal.

KEV (*offering* BREN*'s money back to him*). I'd pay rent for the room.

BREN. Just get a job Kev – that'd sort you out – right – come on – I've to go to work!

ANDY. Well you won't be getting any Christmas presents from me Bren – I'll tell you that much — you're as mean.

BREN. I don't care – will you just go please?

ANDY. We mightn't be seeing each other for a while Bren – you know? And I mean he (*indicates Kev*) might throw himself in the river this weekend – he's so depressed. And the oul fella's wetting the bed. He could be crashing his car into a wall right now – d'you know what I mean?

BREN. And what about Gordon – what's he doing right now – do you think?

ANDY. . . . That's not funny.

BREN. Just go – will you? Come on – I need to get ready.

ANDY (*to* KEV). . . . Do you think he'll forgive me – Gordon? I mean when he grows up – forgiveness and all that?

KEV. Yeah – I think he will.

ANDY. It's just – you know – I think he'll be happier there – they have everything.

KEV. Yeah.

ANDY. . . . And I'll be able to phone him and stuff – I'm sure.

KEV. Yeah.

ANDY. I mean he'll be happier down there – to give him a chance like – you know? They've a swing in the garden and toys.

BREN. Jesus – will you just go – please – come on – I've things to do.

ANDY. Right I'm going – I'm going. (*Pause.*) Are you sure you don't want to go out for a pint tonight Kev, cos I mean we could just have a quiet few – somewhere local – you know? – just the two of us – like – I mean – I know a bloke – a mate of mine – like we could kip on his floor like – like – if you want like.

KEV. Yeah – I – know – I think – actually, I think I'm not going to go back to Galway. I'm just going to head over there instead – home – I mean – like – what's the worst Da can say to me? I mean – if I'm there – he'll just have to talk – you have to be able to talk – like today like – the way we talked and I'll talk to him some more and you know – I'll be there to help – talk and I mean he could tell me where Mam is as well and I could go over and see her – see if she wants to talk as well like . . . forgiveness and expressing yourself cos otherwise people don't know what's going on in your head? That'd work – wouldn't it?

ANDY. Can you boil an egg?

KEV. I mean – I'd leave him his privacy and all that – that's if he's staying there.

ANDY. He likes it soft-boiled.

KEV. Here's your money back.

BREN. No – no – you keep it Kev.

KEV. Thanks.

BREN (*to* KEV). Right well it was good to see you Kev. Mind yourself.

ANDY (*to* BREN). We should do that – some time – go for a drink – talk about things – Bren – you know – will we do that?

BREN. I've to go to fucking work!

ANDY. All right – fair enough – that's it – no more calling to your door, no more disputes, no more Christmas presents – all right?

BREN. Yeah okay – right – see you.

ANDY. Sorry for bleeding on your carpet.

BREN. Yeah okay – right.

ANDY. See you Bren.

BREN. Yeah.

KEV. See you.

ANDY *and* KEV *exit. The door shuts behind them. Pause. BREN exits into the kitchen with the towel and enters again. He gathers his thoughts for a moment then sits down by the computer and looks out beyond the room. There is a sense, now that he is alone, that he is free to show some outward signs of the impact of the last few hours. Pause. He gets up and exits into the bathroom. He enters from the bathroom with a toilet roll. He places the toilet roll by the computer and after a moment turns the computer on.*

Lights down.

End.

A Nick Hern Book

Take Me Away first published in Great Britain as a paperback
original in 2004 by Nick Hern Books Limited, 14 Larden Road,
London W3 7ST in association with Rough Magic Theatre Company

Cover image: Alphabet Soup

Typeset by Country Setting, Kingsdown, Kent, CT14 8ES
Printed and bound in Great Britain by Bookmarque, Croydon,
Surrey

A CIP catalogue record for this book is available from
the British Library

ISBN 1 85459 797 3